CRY OF THE ANCIENTS

"Burning of the White Dog"
Used with permission of the U. S. Department
of the Interior (See Chapter 21)

Cry of the Ancients

BY GREY OWL AND LITTLE PIGEON
Illustrated by Daniel Nicholas

Table of Contents

FOREWORD 7

INTRODUCTION 9

SILENT WATCHER 13

CHAPTER 1 . . . . The Call 15

CHAPTER 2 . . . . What Is an Indian? 19

CHAPTER 3 . . . . The Wampum 27

CHAPTER 4 . . . . . . The Missing Wampum 33

CHAPTER 5 . . . . A Search Begins 47

CHAPTER 6 . . . . . . Legends and Traditions 51

CHAPTER 7 . . . The Chickasaw-Choctaw Migration 55

CHAPTER 8 . . Tobacco and the Legend of the Pipe 61

CHAPTER 9 . . . . . The Tradition of the Clans 65

CHAPTER 10 . . The Migration of the Serpent People 71

CHAPTER 11 . . . . The Prophet 75

CHAPTER 12 . . . . The Mounds 81

CHAPTER 13 . . . . . The Ghost Dance Religion 87

CHAPTER 14 . . . . The Code of Handsome Lake 91

CHAPTER 15 . . . . . . Invitation to Scholars 97

CHAPTER 16 . . . . The Case for Israel 105

CHAPTER 17 . . . . The Sacred Name 109

CHAPTER 18 . . . . . . Relics and Inscriptions 117

CHAPTER 19 . . . . Black Hand Gorge 123

CHAPTER 20 . . . . The Long Arm of Coincidence 129

CHAPTER 21 . . . . The Burning of the White Dog 133

CHAPTER 22 . . . . Shadow Memories 137

CHAPTER 23 . . . . The Shadow of Pain 143

CHAPTER 24 . . . . . . The "Savage" Indian 145

CHAPTER 25 . . . . The Extra Witness 155

CHAPTER 26 . . . . . The Hiding of the Sacred Harp 163

CHAPTER 27 . . . . . The Cry of the Ancients 171

CHAPTER 28 . . . . Little Pigeon to the Churches 177

CHAPTER 29 . . . . . . Grey Owl to His People 193

BIBLIOGRAPHY 205

Foreword

Of the American Indians' original philosophy, "there are only veiled hints. What manner of man was he before the advent of white civilization has been left largely to conjecture. . . ." How true! Artifacts, pictures, and white men's tales of the Wild West provide a confusion of images, not the least dramatic being the stories of bloody massacres and outrages against white women and children.

It is mostly out of the struggle of war that the concept of American Indian character and way of life has been presented to white men. Scholars and missionaries have tried to be more accurate and more charitable, but white men are not Indians and understanding is difficult.

Though there have been individual exceptions, it is generally true that the Indian's mind has been inscrutable to the white person and few Indians have done much to bridge the gap themselves.

Modern explorations and scholarship now make it abundantly clear that there has been a rich and fascinating variety of culture in ancient America. Speculations by historians, philosophers, religionists, archaeologists, and laymen have produced thousands of books, pamphlets, pictures, and re-creations of these ancient cultures. Ruins

7

of cities, roads, and agricultural systems are methodically examined. Descriptive literature about American antiquities continues to increase while world-famous scientists representing many institutions probe the past by uncovering the remains.

This book takes note of some of these studies. It includes quotations from reports both old and new. But it is not primarily a modern scholarly treatise. It is more like a review of memory—nostalgic, pathetic, inspiring, moralistic—challenging Indians who are supposed to know about memories recalled by one to join in telling more of what others may know.

In these pages one will find windows opening into the Indian soul. Argue with the data and the conclusions if you like, but look into those windows! Those who do may see many fascinating sights, think new thoughts, and sense a new feeling of appreciation for the inner life of a people who think of themselves as children of God.

Maurice L. Draper

Introduction

When Grey Owl began to assemble the material for this book some twenty years ago, his aim was not to publish but to learn. He had some vague idea that—if the money were ever available—he would send copies of the work to other Indians here and there who might be interested.

At first he was not much concerned with historians and anthropologists except to say that the half-truths they expounded were more dangerous to his people than outright untruths would have been.

If Grey Owl's original plan had been carried out, there would have been no need to offer explanation of who and what he was. Indians would have been quick to recognize his role.

The reasons for my deciding to publish the results of these years of research will develop in the book itself. It now becomes my difficult task to attempt to clarify Grey Owl for other readers. It is difficult because of the particular commitment of his life. Priest or leader he was not—only a man personally and completely dedicated to his people, and by his people he meant all Indians.

When he was six years old, and before the authorities could "capture" him for school, he was taken from his mother and put under the direction of the old men of his tribe in order that he might first learn the wisdom of his fathers. His mother told me of that day. There was a knock at the door and an old man entered. She had looked to this day with a mixture of dread and pride. Offering food and drink to the visitor, she busied herself preparing the bundle of her child's clothing.

The old man spoke only once. When all was ready, he turned to the boy and said, "Go kiss your mother." Those were the last words Grey Owl was to hear his first teacher speak during the four months he lived with him.

His mother, watching, saw the old man stride away. Not once did he look back to see if his charge was following. Sometimes dragging his bundle, sometimes tripping over it, the little boy trudged on, keeping the old man in sight.

How cruel that sounds today. Yet Grey Owl said that of all his teachers that old one had the best lesson of all to teach. By his silence, the boy's perception was aroused. When they arose in the morning, the old man would begin to lay out the tools that would serve their task for the day. At first the clues to their occupation would be plain and easy to understand. An ax and a small hatchet meant chopping firewood. A purse and a basket—they were going to the store. As time went on, the preparations became more subtle, but the boy was learning to use his eyes; his understanding increased until he grew to sense a man's plan of action at the first small move.

There were other teachers during the following three years. He learned the ancient rituals, the old customs, and sat for hours listening to stories of a past long dead before

10

the white man came. He learned the languages of neigh-
boring tribes, the Delaware and Chippewa; how to send his
mind away when he was hurt, and how to "disappear" by
standing very still.

These things he learned before he knew one word of
English. Why they singled out this little boy, so very
young, is now unknown, for all his teachers have departed.
Perhaps because of the particular line from which he
came—perhaps in the old tradition, they recognized the
clay they had to work with.

At any rate, I hope they know how well their work
was done. As a young man he made a private and very
personal commitment of his life to seek out knowledge for
his people.

Specifically, the experiment in which he was engaged
was to learn whether it is possible for an Indian to survive
in the white man's world and still keep faith with his own
kind. It was a task that involved his family but such was
the charm of this man that we leaped joyfully and with
unflagging enthusiasm into the years of poverty and of
isolation from our people.

His vow was to bring honor to God and self-respect to
his brothers. He was so determined that no honor or
benefit should come to him that he took the name Grey
Owl—which is not his tribal name.

This, to do him justice in his commitment, is all that
we can tell of his life—he loved his people.

Little Pigeon

11

Silent Watcher

As a child beside the curbstone
   Watching each parade that passes
Is the Redman in his homeland.
   All the color and the fanfare,
All the banners flying gaily,
   All the heavy tanks and mortars,
All the wealth and might of nations
   Pass before his wondering glances.
Quite secure upon his curbstone
   Sits the child of nature, marveling,
Knowing deep within his spirit
   Still Earth-Mother soon will call him.
"Come, my child, for this is over.
   Come into the hills and forests.
Let me show you greater glories—
   How the fern-leaf curls in springtime,
How the moon glows on the water;
   How to raise your arms at dawning
Drawing deep the air of freedom.
   Come and watch with me at sunset
All the banners of your father,
   Mighty Sky-Chief; all his colors
Flung across the great lodge doorway.

"I will whisper and assure you
   Of the love we bear each other.
By the Sky-Chief's rain you thirst not;
   From my harvests I will feed you;
From the fields and from the forests
   Medicine to heal your illness.
For your spirit all the glory—
   The security of knowing
You are safely with your parents.
   Rest, my child, the day is over."

                   Little Pigeon

CHAPTER 1

The Call

For what, my people, do we hunger? When the stranger offers us bread, why do we turn on him in bitter pride and cry, "It is a stone. Away with it!"

When one comes fawning and says insidiously, "Oh, I know the Indian and his glory—how he could ride and fight and hunt; how cunning on the trail of his enemy; how canny his nature lore; how true and enduring his friendship," what is this reticence that lifts our heads and whispers in our hearts, "You never knew us"?

And those who come wringing their hands, crying aloud the guilt of their ancestors for taking the lands of the "first and true Americans." Why do we stiffen and draw back from their vain apologies? What is this faint stirring of grief—this half-forgotten memory of something infinitely more precious than the land? Think, my brothers, and remember. Open your eyes, Old Ones, and wake from your dreaming. Wake and remember your fathers and the true glory of your past. Do not stop with the history books where one man's opinion caught your people in a small moment and left you there impaled upon a fragment of time.

Back—back beyond the wars and the hatred and the

hunger. Back—beyond the days of your wanderings when your instinct for survival made of you the greatest naturalists of all the world. Back—into the farthest reach of legend. Pause, and listen with your heart.

For I say to you, my brothers—the greatness of the Indian was not that he held the land and roamed free. Today other men hold that land and freedom—yet they often envy and seek that peculiar "something" that has kept your spirits free and proud.

Neither was the glory of the Indian his wild racing of ponies across the plains nor the deftness of canoe paddles on the white water. Come, my brothers, let us open the door to memory; but carefully, for beyond is a glory blinding in its truth.

I call to you, Lakota, whom men call by another name. Whence came you when you drove your laden canoes up the Mississippi and its tributaries? From the south you came, you people of the Serpent, and to the south returned and came again.

I call to you, Shawnee—ask of your old men. Were their fathers not in Florida when the white men first entered the land? And were they not then resting from their migrations from farther south and west?

I call to you, Oneida—you people of the Standing Stone—search your legends and traditions. Trace your generations backward from New York through the rich Ohio country and its mounds, down the Mississippi and its valleys to the great Gulf. Follow its curve and find the land of the Standing Stone and your glory.

Chickasaw—well you know of your beginnings and the dream that brought you safely from the land of sunset.

16

All you nations, search your legends. For they hold the key that can give you back what no man can promise you, no matter how great his sincerity or how rich his purse. Open the door and find your identity as a nation of people. Come to the remembrance of your fathers. Look upon Tula the golden and the days of your innocence.

For in those days, the Great Chief of Heaven spoke to us—to us, the gay and beautiful, the laughing, industrious, rejoicing, adventuring sons of the land—and called us His children. He sent His beloved, the Morning Star, the Healer, to teach us to live in love together.

Where are the Old Ones who could tell of our downfall in those ancient days? In the fair land where the bounties of the Supreme Being were spread for all men, jealousy, greed, and suspicion possessed the people until each man's hand was lifted against his neighbor and the land became one vast battlefield. And the Great Father-of-all looked upon His children with sadness and the prophecy was given:

"This is my fair land. With my hands and my heart have I made it and it is dearer to me than all the lands of earth. If you cannot live by my laws, sharing in the gifts that I have given, then I will cause such enemies as you have never seen to come upon you, and they will put their feet upon your necks and grind your faces in the dust."

But there was a promise, too. Remember?

"Some far day you will begin to lift your heads, and you will climb to the mountain and lift your arms saying as one voice, 'Father, we are here!' And I will remember."

17

Now, as a people we are called to awaken. But one man says come this way and another, that way. "Come into the light of Civilization," says one. "Learn to fight for your 'rights' and take as other men do."

"No," says another, "you are prettier if you stay in the tepee, tan your own leather and make fire with sticks." Which shall we choose, my brothers, as we come into the promise?

Let us first strip away the clutter that the storybooks have included about our past. For this is wisdom: If a man lose all he has—his wealth, his country, his hopes—and still may keep his secure knowledge of himself and his worth as a link in the chain of life, he has a rock to build upon.

If all things be added unto him—wealth, position, fame, and power—and he have not the anchor of his heritage, he is an empty canoe upon the waters of life.

So let us with our memories first seek our heritage— our lovely past. I have a little knowledge; you, my brothers, have more.

Let us lift our heads and our voices, for it is time.

Grey Owl

CHAPTER 2

What Is an Indian?

Over the years the American Indian has been greatly misrepresented. According to fanciful accounts he was unfailingly brave; a real dead-eye-Dick on the trail; honest and true; treacherous and sly; dirty (since the pioneers "could smell one a mile away"); romantic; ignorant; possessed of some mysterious cult of knowledge; and a devil to his women.

Because they were human these qualities might have been found in some of the people some of the time but they could hardly have been characteristic of all of the people all of the time.

Most of the knowledge the white man garnered about the Indian came through the painful experience of war. War, of necessity, must color one's opinion of the enemy. It is unrealistic to picture oneself at war with a child of God. It is much more palatable if one is convinced the enemy is a bestial savage, even though there may be a grudging respect for his ability.

Actually, the Indian did very little to correct these impressions. Neither before nor after the coming of the white man did the Indian try to win converts to his way of life or to his religion. In fact, events in his past taught him to be reticent about sharing the most sacred aspects of his life. Rituals were carefully guarded, old traditions repeated only in the secret medicine societies.

There were few, a very few, of the early settlers whom the Indian learned to respect and to trust, but even to these he could not speak of his ancient, sacred beliefs.

He was a past master of war in the wilderness and he had his own rules. What a shock it must have been to the gallant French and English to encounter an enemy who crept through the trees rather than march like gentlemen to their death!

The centuries before the white man came had been filled with warfare. All were "holy wars," earnestly and carefully prepared for by purification and sacrifice—an idea not without its parallels. If an individual survived at all, it was because he was a bit more resourceful and wily than his enemy. Luck had little to do with it and superior weapons even less. Yes, in warfare the Indian was brave, resourceful, and wily. But one must remember that he had a real "Holy Cause"—he was fighting for his land, his homes, and his way of life.

As for the smell, quite probably it was obvious—a mixture of woodsmoke, bear grease, and leather. However, one must remember that the pioneer undoubtedly did not smell so sweet to the Indian either.

The Indians were a people steeped in survival lore. In a day when most do not know boneset from dandelion, their knowledge of food plants and medicinal herbs seems incredible.

But more than this, they developed certain admirable traits of character that were as essential to survival as that knowledge of food and medicine. Children were taught self-control at an early age. Imagine the disaster if one had to calm a temper tantrum while trying to conceal a child from the enemy. The acceptance of pain until it could be relieved was important to a people without a handy bottle of aspirin. Utter and complete loyalty was not just admirable, it was essential.

What about the attitude toward women? There have been so many misunderstandings. It is not wise to generalize too much, since customs varied from an almost matriarchal society to a polygamous one. If one pictures the Indian male lolling about the fire while his poor, broken-down wife does all the work, it is an example of misunderstanding. Today if hubby goes hunting, he hops downtown to equip himself with a hunting license, the proper weapon, and shells. He loads into his car a portable tent, or at least a good, dry sleeping bag, a camp stove, and a supply of groceries in case his luck fails.

In the old days, hubby first made his bow, his spear, and a supply of points. The work of preparation was constant, unending, and very hard on the hands. He kept his hunting gear to the minimum, however, anticipating a much heavier load on the way back.

All was not roses on the trail, either. Through rain, sleet, and snow, he hiked in soggy moccasins, always keeping a wary eye out for enemy war parties. If he found signs of them, it was sometimes expedient to conceal himself beneath a dripping bush to take his rest. After all this, plus the heavy load carried on the homeward trek, one would hardly expect the little woman to hand him a hoe and order him to work when he returned to the

21

village. And she didn't. Children streamed forth to meet him. Eager hands divested him of his burden and bent to the skinning.

It is hardly conceivable either that he would come in storming, "This place is a mess!" In many tribes the lodge belonged to the woman, and what she did with it was her business. His job was to provide meat for the table and hides for the tanning. Considering that it took several weeks to tan buckskin, a wife would have known that her warrior-hunter could not find the time to be responsible for this part of the labor. It is true that all men were not skilled in the art of arrow making and hunting, but each had to produce something with which to trade.

While the physical world of the Indian is fairly accurately pictured, all the artifacts in all the museums of the world cannot reveal the Indian's thoughts. We know fairly well the way he built his various homes, how he hunted, fished, and made fire. In late years we even begin to see the Indian wars in better perspective. Modern sociologists have pointed to the sorry results of poverty, disease, and alcoholism, but we know now that, far from being a vanishing race, Indians are on the increase.

However, of his original philosophy, there are only veiled hints. What manner of man he was before the advent of white civilization has been largely left to conjecture; yet many of the first settlers left writings describing the Indian as he was in their day.

Let us examine some of them. Surely we will admit that Christopher Columbus saw the real, original article. In his account to his royal sponsors regarding his first landing in America, he said,

22

"I swear to your majesties that there is not a better people in the world than these; more affectionate, affable and mild. They love their neighbors as themselves. Their language is the sweetest, the softest and the most cheerful, for they always speak smiling."—Timothy R. Jenkins, *The Ten Tribes of Israel!*, pp. 103-104.

In one instance an old man approached Columbus and presented a basket of fruit. He said,

"You are come to this country with a force against which, were we inclined to resist, resistance would be folly. We are all, therefore, at your mercy. But if you are men subject to mortality like ourselves, you cannot be unapprised, that after this life there is another, wherein a different portion is allotted to good and bad men. If, therefore, you expect to die, and believe with us, that everyone is to be rewarded in a future state according to his conduct in the present, you will do no hurt to those who do none to you."—Bryan Edwards, *History of the British Colonies, in the West Indies,* Vol. 1, p. 72.

In the year 1620 the Reverend Mr. Cushman said in a sermon preached at Plymouth,

"The Indians are said to be the most cruel and treacherous people in all these parts, even like lions, but to us they have been like lambs, so kind, so submissive and trusty; as a man truly said, many Christians are not so kind or sincere. Though when we came first into this country we were few, and many of us very sick, and many died by reason of the cold and wet, it being the depth of winter . . . when there were not six able persons among us, and the Indians . . . might in one hour have made dispatch of us; yet . . . they never offered us the least injury in

23

word or deed. And by reason of one Tisquanto, that lives among us, and can speak English, we have daily commerce with their kings, and can know what is done or intended toward us among the savages."—Jenkins, pp. 105, 106.

When I was a child in school, I read about "Squanto" and somehow received the impression that it was because he spoke English that he helped the colonists. But as I listened to and observed our customs, I came to realize that these were aids extended to all strangers of goodwill and that in those days it was impossible to eat and know that any around were hungry.

James Adair was a pioneer and Indian trader who came to America about 1735. For forty years he traveled from north to south among Indians and lived with them as a friend and brother. Before he died in 1782, he published a book called *The History of American Indians.* It is accepted as a "faithful and valuable contribution" to American literature, in spite of the fact that he was convinced the Indians were descendants of Israel.

He wrote,

"It is a very difficult thing to divest ourselves, not to say, other persons, of prejudices and favourite opinions; and I expect to be censured by some, for opposing commonly received sentiments. . . . But, TRUTH is my object. . . .

"From the most exact observations I could make in the long time I traded among the American Indians, I was forced to believe them lineally descended from the Israelites. . . ."—Adair, p. 13.

Alvin Colton, writing of the Iroquois in his book, *Origin of the American Indians* (London, 1833), said:

"Their great men, both sachems and captains, are generally poorer than the common people; for they affect to give away and distribute all the presents or plunder they get in their treaties, or in war, so as to leave nothing to themselves. There is not a man in the ministry of the Five Nations who had gained his office otherwise than by merit. There is not the least salary, or any sort of profit annexed to any office, to tempt the covetous or the sordid; but on the contrary, every unworthy action is attended with the forfeiture of their commission."

Another historian observed,

"They are very loving to one another; if several came to a Christian's house, and the master of it gave to one of them victuals and none to the rest, he would divide it into equal shares among his companions. If the Christian visited them they would give them the first cut of their victuals. They never ate the hollow of the thigh of anything they killed; and if a Christian stranger came to one of their houses in their towns, he was received with the greatest hospitality, and the best of everything was set before him."— Smith's *History of New Jersey,* p. 130.

So we find many of our preconceived notions going up the smoke of the campfire.

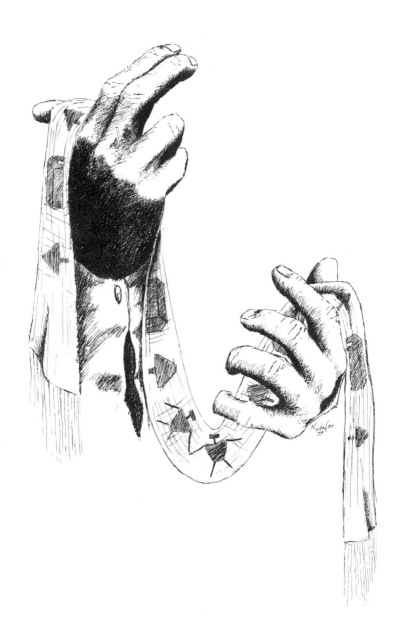

CHAPTER 3

The Wampum

Historians insist that the Indian had no written history. Indians smile and wonder what kind of writing the white man is looking for.

Even a child's first book on Indian lore is full of clues to refute the statement. If an Indian says, "My grandfather told me," it means that the statement he is making is infallibly true. This leads one to suppose he must have a certain respect for his ancestors.

If the historian is looking for a record on paper written letter by letter, word by word, as we write in English, he will be gratified to learn that he is right. There is no such record. However, most Indians did keep a record in one fashion or another, the most graphic and detailed being the wampum. In this context, the word refers to the belts or strips into which the beads were woven.

It seems strange that so few have stumbled on the significance of the wampum. Most people are led to believe that it was money. The individual beads were, it is true, much sought after. The shells from which wampum beads were made were hard to come by—it was much harder still to work these shells into beads.

If an Indian were entering a solemn treaty or making a pledge of peace or war, he accompanied his words with the presentation of a wampum belt. Why? Obviously it must have had some special meaning for him. Beaded belts were not in fashion in those days and would have had no value for the white man. If a pledge of money were needed, the Indian would have brought beaver skins, which *were* used as currency in colonial times.

Woven into the strips were patterns or "ideagraphs." It is not easy to learn to read them. They do have one advantage, however. They do not have to be translated. They are actually "thought patterns" and can be read in any language, if they are read at all.

An Indian might have brought a belt as a pledge which tells the story of a grandfather who had performed some service for his people. In effect he was saying, "On the honor of my ancestors, I promise you. . . ."

In order to appreciate the great value of the wampum's history one must remember the difficulty in obtaining the shells, fashioning them into beads, and finally weaving the belt. One soon realizes a man wouldn't necessarily merit having his name recorded on the wampum for just any old thing. I say "necessarily" because not much of anything seemed to be happening in some of the belts. Not every ancestor did some astonishingly brave deed—but *every generation was represented.*

One thing is missing conspicuously in Indian history—a dating system. The story of one man's life may record a flood, a famine, or a migration, but it will contain no dates. The clue lies in the fact that when the wampum is read at the death of a chief, the readers begin with the chief preceding the deceased and go back generation by generation.

The wampum served the dual purpose of preserving an honorable record of one's ancestors and also accounting for the passage of time.

How long a span of time which has been recorded by this method may be estimated by the fact that in at least one tribe, to my knowledge, teams of men reading without interruption for nine days and nine nights were required to complete the history. And it was a rare generation that required more than a belt or two to tell its part of the story.

Over the years, I have found that this statement provokes predictable reactions and comments from an audience:

1. Quote an acceptable authority—author's name, publisher, volume, and page.
2. If such a record exists, it should be in a museum to protect it.
3. Why don't you see if you can smuggle out a strip or two to prove your statement?

Let me respond, point by point.

1. I am an authority, and so are tens of thousands of Indians who have seen the wampum and heard it read. Consider how published works of history are prepared. Earnest students read and research earlier writers' conclusions and accept their statements made in a previous decade because this writer in turn has quoted an earlier one. At last when enough people have said it, the theory is accepted as a fact. Fair

enough under restricted circumstances, but hardly to be compared with the account of an eyewitness.

Actually the wampum of one tribe has been deciphered and published. Whether all the events are in proper order perhaps no one will ever know, but it fills a large volume. I refer to the wampum of the Delaware Nation called the *Walam Olum* or *Red Score,* translated by Père Christine Rafinesque in 1820, and published by the Indiana Historical Society. It has been read with interest by some and branded a hoax by many.

To the Indians, their wampum is sacred, not to be profaned by those of little faith. They say, "Why should we care whether the white man believes or disbelieves? It is *our* history, and for us it is enough."

2. Many relics have come to light and been relegated to the subterranean chambers of museums, disappeared into private collections, or simply disappeared altogether. What is the reason? Quite often because they present evidence contrary to established opinion and are hard to classify. Could we consign our sacred history to such a fate? Such suggestions are received with horror. It is precisely because the wampum has been guarded so jealously that it has survived. The white man has taken everything else. We would ask, would they also take this?

3. This question requires a great deal of background information before it can be answered. The following information should help.

First, I would suggest a simple experiment. The beautiful book of the *Red Score* is, I believe, a limited edition. Nevertheless, it *is* a published work, and for the time it will serve our purpose.

If you can obtain a copy, read it objectively—but read it from back to front. We have become so used to an orderly procession of dates that it is awkward for us to read without them. Our minds will accept the idea of beginning with one million B.C. and progressing through the milestones of geologic ages—or of beginning with 4000 B.C. and era by era tracing man's search for truth.

But to read a history with no dates is a challenge. Try starting with the first page of the Delaware wampum. It is like floundering in a morass of events with no point of reference, no landmark from which to begin.

Turn to the very last page, the last sentence. Imagine that sentence a strip of beadwork, a wampum belt. Notice that the sentence or brief paragraph is the identification for a particular time period. That last generation has a definite focal point in time.

Now try reading backward, belt by belt. The trail is dim for us today. The names of the rivers are changed; the descriptions of the various camping places mean nothing to us now. But still, west, north, south, and east remain, and the borders of time flow backward, chief by chief.

CHAPTER 4

The Missing Wampum

"INDIANS SEEK RETURN OF WAMPUM" was the headline on a recent newspaper clipping. I began to read, expecting another tongue-in-cheek account of the proposed settlement of some claim.

My first reaction to the account was shock; this proceeded into indignation and at last a blazing fury. I had thought the wampum was intact. Now I learned that in some strange transaction, a series of belts covering the period 1700-1800 wound up in the possession of the New York State University Museum at Albany. The twenty-seven belts valued at $280,000 were acquired "in almost all cases" by purchase.

The Onondaga want them back, and the state says no. Some background information may provide some insights into the significance of this request.

The Iroquois Federation *is*—not was—a formal, well-organized confederation of six nations. History takes the position that the league was formed to increase the strength of the tribes in warfare and indeed, regardless of the purpose the old ones had in mind, it did have that effect, since "in union there is strength."

I have a copy of the Iroquois constitution prepared by the Akwesasne Councilor Organization on the St. Regis Reservation in New York. It has been accepted for use in the public schools of that state. Its every word cries out for peace and law.

Consider:

"It is provided thus: The confederate Sachems have now planted a tree of great peace. . . .

"It is provided thus: A root of four branches has grown out of this tree of great peace—one to the north, one to the south, one to the east, another to the west. Its nature is peace and charity and if any nation or individual outside of the confederacy shall adopt the laws of the great peace, discipline their minds and spirits to obey and honor the wishes of the imperial council fire of the Confederacy, they are welcome to take shelter under its spreading branches."

And again:

"It is provided thus: the confederate Sachems now pull out a pine tree by the roots and into the depths of the hole where the roots were, we gather and throw all weapons of strife and plant again the tree. Thus we establish the Great Peace and hostilities shall not be seen nor heard any more among you, but peace shall be preserved among the united nations."

The Iroquois were committed to this document. Assailed from without, they have been mighty warriors; the law of the Great Peace being threatened, they rose as one. But the spirit of union has been so strong among them, it passed out of the realm of politics and became a spiritual union so firm that even today, meeting as strangers in far-flung places, we say, "I am one of the Six" and know a lift of heart as of brothers reunited.

Who are the Onondaga and why should they be so concerned about these wampum belts?

From the Constitution:

> "Wampum—it is provided thus: the business of the confederated nations shall be transacted by two combined groups of Sachems. First the Mohawks and Senecas, and second the Cayugas, Oneidas, and Tuscaroras. In all cases the decisions and resolutions of the Confederate council shall be referred to the fire-keepers, the Onondagas, for final confirmation.
>
> "Wampum—it is provided thus: When a matter or question is submitted to the council of the Six Nations, it shall be considered by the Mohawks and Senecas first and whatever their decision shall be, it shall be submitted to the second combined groups of Sachems. Their decision shall then be returned to the first house. If they agree unanimously, the business is reported to the fire-keepers for confirmation."

Now, beyond any shadow of doubt, the sale or transfer of twenty-seven wampum belts would have required the unanimous consent of all the tribes. As fire-keepers, the Onondaga would have been responsible for the final—but only the final—word. Add to this the fact that the "center place" of the Iroquois is at the Onondaga settlement, and one can imagine the concern of the present chiefs.

As to how the transfer came about—ah, that is a moot question. Under what possible combination of circumstances would the councils sanction the creation of a gap of one hundred years in the record?

In my initial shock, I entertained some hard suspicions. Someone must have succeeded at last in filching the records. The constitution provides too many safeguards guaranteeing the dedication and devotion of the Sachems to believe that they would give up willfully so important a series. Surely the belts had been stolen—and that would put the state of New York in an awkward position.

These were my thoughts as I began to seek for the answers. Only superficial research was required to unearth the story. Apparently the sale was legal. Signed, sealed, and delivered with great ceremony, the belts had passed from the possession of the heirs of the confederacy to the Museum of the University of New York.

Apparently it was legal. But as to the nature of the transaction, it would depend upon one's own particular viewpoint.

As Indians, we have been subjected to apologies *ad nauseum* for "the dirty deal" our ancestors got. So many white Americans have vilified the early settlers for "taking the lands of the first and true Americans" that we often wonder if these lands have become a millstone about their necks. In vain we protest, "It wasn't just the land—it was the constant broken promises. It was the slick political moves we couldn't understand, much less forgive."

They stare at us blankly. What on earth could we have had to lose except the land we stood upon, they seem to wonder. Perhaps if, in some small way, the white man could be helped to understand, even the loss of the wampum would be an acceptable price to pay.

I ask you once more to use your imagination. It will be very hard because all your values will be at cross purposes.

Imagine. . . .

You have a government that, for all your complaints

36

about it, is your choice of all the governments of earth.

You are devout in your religion. You are Roman Catholic, Methodist, Presbyterian, or any one of dozens of other faiths, but you truly believe you love and serve God.

You also have a favorite doctor in whom, with good reason, you have confidence.

You have other customs and traditions that make up your way of life, but these three things are most important to you. In the observance of these three you have learned from generations back certain rituals. You know that at a certain time you are privileged to choose your leaders in government. You register, you campaign, you vote. You present your views and complaints at the proper time. You may do this or not as you choose, for that is part of your freedom.

In your religion, there are rites that are very precious to you. Some of them are administered only to your own congregation. It is your way and you feel uplifted and comforted in their observance.

Even in your medicine, you enjoy the freedom to choose. You and the doctor get along well together. He knows you and you have complete trust in him. You may gripe about the long wait in his reception room, but after all it's worth waiting just to see him grin and hear him say, "Take this. You're doing fine."

So now . . .

Incredible as it may seem, your country is attacked by another nation. And fantastically, incredibly, you lose the war.

A new government is set up. No more President. No more Senate or House of Representatives. Not even a city council or even the old standby, the dogcatcher. The affairs of government are handled by a Supreme Council—impossibly alien and far away. Even at the local level, the officials are strangers. They speak another language. They look upon your gatherings with suspicion.

As for your religion, they have locked up the churches. They scoff at your "childish beliefs." They make crude jokes about your kneeling, and prayer has been declared unlawful.

As for the family doctor, he also is taboo. You are given a number and you present yourself at a clinic. You are run through an assembly line of robot-faced clinicians who stare through you and fling you out on the other side.

That's phase one. Now for phase two.

You still can't have a real government or open assembly, but you gather in neighborhood groups to talk over the good old days. You remember the great men of the past, and the names of those who were powerful in industry or in government have a pleasant ring because they remind you of your own lost glory: Washington, Lincoln, Roosevelt, Garner, Goldwater, Truman; the warriors—Eisenhower, MacArthur, Rickenbacker.

You remember the Gettysburg Address and the Bill of Rights and secretly you teach them to your children—and the Star Spangled Banner and the Battle Hymn of the Republic.

As for that newfangled clinic—you are so uncomfortable there, you feel worse when you come out than when you went in. So—you find your old doctor in a shabby corner and he does the best he can for you and it is very good.

Phase three.

The new government seems to awaken to the fact that you're still in existence. You become something of a curiosity to the thousands of aliens pouring in to take up the business of the country.

Probably the most agonizing aspect of this period is your fear that you are losing your children. The enemy— for he is still that, to you—has set up schools and academies where your children are beyond your reach. They are learning alien doctrines and values and their memories of the old beliefs and customs are growing dim. You long for your young with an aching hunger, and tell yourself they are not really lost but strayed.

As for the new people, they still can't quite fathom the fact that you have minds or that your old-time beliefs have any merits. But they have plumbed the depths of their great intelligence and have come up with a doctrine that is to become the guideline for all their machinations.

"Verily, it is sad that this people has lost its culture. No longer do they remember the great things of their past.

"Therefore, let there be museums upon the land and let us gather together all the relics and the tools of this people for our edification.

"Let us gather all the implements of worship and the rituals by which they profess to worship their gods, being careful not to delude the public into seeing any virtue or merit in such folklore."

Now you are the folk people. Your memories and your faith are precious to you and all you have left of your glory is the reciting of them to each other and to your children when possible—and this at the risk of public ridicule. So, when the new rulers ask you for these precious things, you hang your head and agree that you have forgotten.

How to get at the truth?

"Go to, and let us find one of the folk people who understands our need to know. Let us convince him how great and beautiful is the museum and then let us send him to seek entrance to the secret meetings and in this way we will gain his trust. It is right that we do this inasmuch as the folk people are too ignorant to preserve their own documents."

Their task is not too difficult. In the academies are many of your bright young men. Some have adapted to the new regime more easily than others. Some have begun to understand the drive for advancement that characterizes the alien society. And there are a few who have this modern quality of ambition and long to draw the rest of their people with them. It is perhaps the most common human motivation that directs both the young man and the people who hire him: he is thinking of the possible future benefits to himself and his people; they are thinking of the increase of their own knowledge. Notice that until now neither of them is guilty of any great sin. We might say they are engaged in a noble pursuit. But let us see how it works out.

It will take time for the young man to convince you of his sincerity, but at last you believe him and he is welcomed into your secret meetings. Let us suppose that the ritual to which he is invited is Holy Communion, and let us suppose that since he has spent most of his young life in the academy, this is his first exposure to this old and

40

honored sacrament. How joyfully you receive him into the fold!

He sits in the back corner of the room and jots his notes hurriedly, for he is to describe the ceremony fully at a later date.

"Many people here—20 or 30 maybe. Mostly families. Some single. Pretty quiet. Chairs in rows. 2 men go front. Light candles. . . . Some men, I think 3 or 4, go up front.

"Something on table. Can't see because covered. Secret charms?

"All people stand, sing. 'Wholly! Wholly!' (Sic) Some crying. Man in front says something but I can't hear because his head is lowered and voice muffled. More singing—something about breaking bread. (Is this old expression mng to eat together?)

"All kneel on floor—hard to write now. Object on table uncov. Seems to be silver tray. Man pass it to people. Bits of bread. Each takes piece and eats. (Maybe symbolic of old times when food was plentiful?)

"More singing. Missed words because dropped papers. All kneel. Man passes tray with sm. glasses wine.

"Later. Summary: I expected this to be prelude to a feast or orgy as we have heard of, but not much else happened. People shook hands or kissed and left soon after. This is possibly a ritual of brotherhood—hence breaking bread together. Or may be remains of nature cult. As wheat and fruit of the vine symbolic."

Now locked away in some secret, well-guarded vault are your Constitution, the Declaration of Independence, the casualty lists of your beloved dead, the things you treasure of your history. You have kept them safe from those who would scoff at them.

But your situation is growing more desperate. Your people are being divided. In the schools, your children are growing up with no true knowledge of the old ways, and everything you say is twisted out of shape. Sometimes the misinterpretations of your customs are quite innocent, sometimes they are deliberate, but it seems that you will never be able to make yourselves understood. And at that precise psychological moment, someone happens to touch the raw nerve that makes you leap to do their bidding.

"It will help the new people understand! They will see that you are people, too."

Awake! This has not been an imagined course of events. This is how it happened. Not just in the instance of the wampum, though this is a classic case. The only difference is that you have been for this brief time a part of the "folk people."

It was during that era, in such a climate, that libraries began to fill with dissertations on the "lore of the Indian." Every historian competed to define the Indian way of life and each had his stable of "informants," as he called them. Museums accumulated such a plethora of arrowheads, baskets, pottery, canoes, cradle boards, tomahawks, and other gear that they are able to draw from their store-houses even today a wealth of material for new exhibits.

The picture that emerged was that of a race which had existed in a vacuum with no experience save the day-to-day scrabble for existence—a race without literature, history, or invention.

42

The purely social festivities were explained as sacred mysteries:

"Look! This savage people worships the otter...."

Where the real worship was observed, it was explained as something the Indian had borrowed from the white man.

Perhaps the league chiefs thought the wampum would stem the tide.

"See—we are men! We have a record."

Instead—there are the belts, stagnant in a glass case, satisfying no one except as a curiosity.

Now let us return to the arguments between the tribal leaders and the New York State Department of Education, for in them we go a step further in the search for truth.

Says the Onondaga chief:

"They've got the belts and can't read them. We can make use of them. What good is there if they keep them?"

The State Education Department protests, "The belts represent political events rather than religion."

The Onondaga: "Our religion and our laws are intertwined."

The so-called "Indian authorities" protest that they do not believe the Indians can read the belts. They have tried repeatedly to find someone who can read them and to date they have found no one who can consistently do this.

Hoh! my brothers! You hold faithful!

The woods are full of "authorities" by virtue of reading many books or of living among us for a few years. To many of them we have opened our hearts only to come to the sad conclusion, "You never knew us."

Perhaps you have to have come down the ages as an

Indian—to have experienced the loss of your past glory, to be branded a savage or a fool—to understand.

Many things we reveal to those who seem sincerely interested, *but the wampum has never been read in the presence of an outsider.* This is so firmly ingrained into the national character that it sets up a mental block even to think of it. Even among ourselves, the belts were not taken out to be read as a book on a winter's evening. It was part of the character of the wampum from ages past that it be read only to the initiated and only on certain solemn occasions.

And it is this very arrogance of the "authorities" which has put a stumbling-block in the path of communication.

"*We* do not know it; therefore, it does not exist."

"*They* will not answer our questions; therefore, they do not know."

"Ask an Indian what he knows about the old people, the mounds, the cities, and you get blank stares and a shrug—therefore, they do not remember."

How shall he answer those who have already formed their conclusions? How shall he share the memory of his past when it refutes all the historians have written the past two centuries?

If you are still wondering why this should at last assume such importance to the Indian, how would you like to reach the point where the Lord's Supper is "the remains of a nature cult"? Because the half-truth is taught as truth in the schools, portrayed on film, preached to our young, and displayed graphically in all the museums of the world, we tend ourselves to forget that there was more to it than now meets the eye.

44

The wampum so displayed has taught no one anything, except that "the Indian 'did' beadwork." It has not increased the understanding of scholars to realize that whether we "read" by interpreting letters or symbols, so long as the meaning comes through to the reader it is an effective method. Thus, the original contract was unfulfilled and one hopes the belts will be returned to those who "can make use of them."

Nevertheless, though my words have been bitter, I have great respect for scholars and for all who seek truth. Let us turn the pages backward to those old, old days and see if we can find the ancient people and their truths.

CHAPTER 5

A Search Begins

The little house was very quiet. Both the beds in the room were filled with sleeping children tumbled together like puppies. On the wide old desk a handbag, intricately rose-carved, was ready for delivery in the morning. Grey Owl had used his day well—and tomorrow, the electric bill would be paid and the house would bloom with lights again.

Tonight the candlelight shone softly on my beads, yellow and red and white. It shone, too, on the book Grey Owl held in his lap. That very morning a neighbor had introduced me to a remarkable invention, the Library Bus, and I had come home loaded to the eyebrows with books. Among them was a very old copy of Howe's *Historical Collections of Ohio.*

About 1825, we learned from this book, a certain farmer dug into a mound near Newark, Ohio, and found a curious stone-lined cavity. He lifted out a small stone case and found inside a bar about nine inches long, also of stone, on which was carved a figure of a man, bearded and robed. On the back and sides were deep scratches which he supposed to be some kind of writing.

47

The account said he took the stone to a Presbyterian minister who thought the writing might be Hebrew; but, as he was not learned, he could not read it. Sometime later, he showed the relic to a Jewish Rabbi in Cincinnati who pronounced it Hebrew indeed, but of a style of writing in use before the Babylonian captivity. The writing appeared to be nine of the Ten Commandments.

Grey Owl had reached that part of the story and fell silent. When I looked up I saw that he had retreated to that land of memory he so often sought.

"What is it?" I asked. "Have you heard of this before?"

"Yes," he replied, "but I didn't know any of them had been found."

There was more to the story, a sequel we were to read again and again in the following years.

The implications of the find were upsetting to many people who saw the Indian as a primitive savage. During this period the whole country was inflamed over the bitter Indian wars, and it was unthinkable that the Indian might have had even the remotest idea of the Ten Commandments.

To the early settlers every little hillock was an Indian mound; ergo, anything in it was Indian. Tomahawks and arrowheads, beads, pottery, and mica the scholars could accept, but a bearded figure with Hebrew inscriptions?

"Bah! Humbug! Hoax!" they cried.

The story so sparked our curiosity that it sent us again and again, years upon years, searching out old books to see if there were any other "finds." As soon as our day's work was done, and the little ones safely in bed, we flew to our books to read and talk far into the night. Many times, something we read would recall some legend or tradition, and we marveled; for here at last were the Ancient People, the Old Ones.

Sadly enough, though we read many accounts of the finding of inscriptions, the relics themselves had often disappeared. Most of them had been turned over to museums, but the unpopularity of the idea sentenced them to obscure corners.

It took us years to find again the little stone figure. We were doubly surprised to find it practically in our own neighborhood, in the museum at Coshocton, Ohio. Daniel, our artist son, was lecturing to the Historical Society there and stood entranced before the case. The curator explained that there were still some doubts as to its authenticity.

Dan grinned impishly. "Oh, it's authentic, all right."

I remembered the conversations among our people when one of them would bring in a newspaper clipping about some scholar's interpretation of a relic.

"Well, they're getting warm," we would chuckle.

THE CRY OF THE ANCIENTS

From the lands of past far distant
Call the ancients to their people.
'Mid the rubble long forgotten
Cry the voices long in slumber.

49

On the winds the whisper travels
Over plains, across the prairies;
Echoing from the great, tall mountains
Far across the flowing rivers.

Thus the cry goes outward, seeking
For the old man and the young man;
For the children born and unborn,
And the women in their labor.

Forget not us who went before you
In your tales around the campfire.
Let us live in all our glory
In the songs that we have taught you.

Thus the ancients cry their message
From the lands of past far distant;
'Mid the rubble long forgotten
Cry their voices long in slumber.

Dan Nicholas

CHAPTER 6

Legends and Traditions

Volumes could be written (and in fact, have been written) recording legends from the many tribes. Still the surface has not been scratched. Students of history become more and more confused as they wander through a world inhabited by animals that speak, little people from under the earth, sky people descending by the rainbow, and ancients teaching precepts the student himself heard in Sunday school.

It may be unfair to select from this mountain of literature only those few that seem to prove our point. However, it must be agreed that this method has precedent. We aren't trying to rewrite all the books; we wish only to point a few directions and send the scholars back to their drawing boards for another look.

It is well to keep in mind that the word "legend" has been sadly misused, like many others. Not all the campfire tales were legend. In the days before radio, TV, and newspapers, winter evenings would have been dreary indeed except for the storyteller.

Often he traveled from tribe to tribe and was greeted enthusiastically. He brought news of relatives in other places and could be depended upon for a store of tales to interest both the old and young. He was fed and given a good seat by the fire. His audience was quick to note the state of his moccasins, or the sorry condition of his coat, and to replace them when it was indicated. They gave him gifts of tobacco, beads, or furs to help him on his journey.

To the children he told stories of how the flowers got their aroma, of why the crow is black, and how the rapids and falls were made by the stamping of the moose. To try to interpret these as some deep philosophy or metaphysical religion is to confuse the issue utterly.

For the young men and women, he had wonderful legends and tales of adventure and romance. Almost invariably these pointed a moral or taught a lesson: if only man would really listen to the voices of nature, he would learn something about himself and his relation to the world in which he lived.

Antoine Simon le Page Dupratz published a *History of Louisiana, Western Virginia and Carolina* in 1763. In it he observed that traditions were preserved by frequent repetitions. Each generation delivered them only to those few young men whose abilities and characters fitted them for the task of preserving them. This is carried on even to the present time by many.

Still, legend is a prettier word and many traditions are called legends by Indians. The difference seems to lie in the fact that legends were told and shared from tribe to tribe, while traditions were held sacred to the particular band and held inviolate and unchangeable.

The origins of many of our traditions are hidden by the mists of time. They have become so much a part of our custom that we no longer question why or how they began. They reflect the life of the "Old People," and when we lay aside old customs to adopt new ways, we feel their brooding presence.

What I have chosen to write are those stories that I personally have heard which have to do with historical or sacred memories.

CHAPTER 7

The Chickasaw - Choctaw Migration

The Chickasaw believe that at one time their ancestors lived far west of a great river. They had a king who had two sons. There are actually two stories which are told about their migration into the Southeast. In one, both the sons were leaders on the journey. In the other, one of them stayed behind. However, both accounts agree on the main particulars, so it might be interesting to consider both. This may also be a case where tradition becomes legend by being translated into the vernacular. The first is found in Jenkins.

Very long ago, the ancestors of the Chickasaw were called Chichimec. Because of many wars, a group of people resolved to leave the country far to the Southwest where they lived. The Beloved Men had told them that in ancient times others of their people had traveled toward the rising sun and had never returned. They were in hopes that somewhere they might come upon the descendants of those who had left them long ago.

They prepared themselves by great rituals and purification and at last the Beloved Men said that God had instructed them to take a rod of a sapling and carry it with them. Wherever they encamped, they should drive it into the ground. If it were bent in the morning, they should continue their journey as the rod indicated. If it should stand upright they would know they had reached their destination. They traveled under the leadership of one of the sons of their king.

So they began their journey to the Eastward, many hundreds of people and their children. At night they made camp, and the rod was set into the ground. In the morning it was seen to incline toward the sunrise as they rose and continued their journey. The days grew into weeks and the weeks into months and always the rod directed them Eastward. Children were born on the trail and sometimes the people grew ill, but strangely none of them died of their sickness. Sometimes the land was dry and parched and the people were faint with thirst. Sometimes the voice of the thunder was heard and they were deluged with rain. Sometimes the people complained that the journey was too long, yet always and ever, the rod bent Eastward.

At last they came to a river so wide, so very wide, it seemed they had reached another sea and the people were afraid. "Our God has led us to our death in the waters," they said, "for see! the rod points Eastward and we shall be drowned."

But the Beloved Men directed them to make boats of the trees and at last they crossed to the other side. They traveled a few days after crossing the great waters and at last came a day when they arose to find the rod standing straight and true and they knew they had found their new land.

The other legend was told to me many years ago by an old man of the Choctaw nation.

In some dim and distant past, in the region of Old Mexico lived a band of Indian people. One time they had great trouble for they were attacked by a stronger and larger race who were very cruel.

Determined to suffer no more, they called a council of all the people. In those days they had a king whose two sons, Chaktat and Chickasak, were chosen to lead the people. But first they had to wait for a dream that would show them the Great Spirit would go with them. At last it came and these were the words spoken by their God:

"My children, I look with favor upon your desires to leave the land of your birth. Erect within the center of your camp a pole. In the morning travel in the direction it points. Keep the pole with you always. When it stands erect, there shall you remain and make your home, for this is the land I have prepared for you."

So the journey began and ever the pole pointed Eastward. They marched for many moons. Often sickness, pain, and weariness afflicted them. But as was their custom, the strong helped the weak. Sometimes they were forced to stop and recover their strength, but the pole remained true to its directing and they would move on. It is said the journey covered forty-three years and the people who had started became old; children born on the trail grew up and had children of their own. A few people died, but their bones were carefully wrapped and carried along so that they, too, would share in the inheritance.

When the journey was nearly over they reached the

shores of a great river. They had never seen a stream so huge and they sank down in dismay.

The Medicine Man spoke. "Brothers, I am an old man and never have my eyes seen so great a body of water. Surely it must have seen many things and is very wise. Still, we follow our pole and it points Eastward, so we must cross. Let us rest here and build rafts. Some of us may die in the crossing, but we follow the Dream. No one knows the beginning or the end of this river, and it belongs to a time beyond the ages of man. Therefore, so that it shall be a memorial for our children, I give it a name. Misha Sipokni it shall be called—beyond the ages, the father of all its kind."

So at last the river was crossed and they traveled many miles beyond its borders. The pole did not stand erect until they had come deep into what is now Mississippi. Here the people separated and became the Choctaw and Chickasaw nations.

There is another story that is told of the migration of the Lenni-Lenape. One version of it is told in an early and rare book, *Inquiry into the Origin of the Antiquities of America* by John Delafield, Jr. (Colt-Burgess & Co.: New York, 1839).

The ancestors of the Lenni-Lenape had lived many hundreds of years before in "a very distant country in the western part of the American continent." Their migrations toward the East led them to the Mississippi and somewhere east of the river they had two encounters that were to change the course of their history.

The first was with Mengies, ancestors of the five

nations who would later reunite to form the Iroquois. This nation also had come a long journey and though both parties were strong in number, they decided to travel together and so increase their strength.

They came at last into a section of country where there were many towns and villages and great fortifications. Here lived the powerful Allegwi among whom, the story says, there were "giants."

It was the Lenape who attempted negotiations for permission to settle in friendship in this rich territory. This the Allegwi refused to grant, but agreed to let the travelers pass through the area and journey eastward.

It was with great consternation that the Allegwi saw the multitude approach and they quickly fortified the towns.

The battle that ensued was long and waged without quarter on either side. Tens of thousands were slain and though first one and then the other would prevail, the blood of all the nations watered the earth for countless miles.

And then at last the remnants of the Lenni-Lenape and their allies won and were free of the fortified places and far to the north and eastward found their home.

CHAPTER 8

Tobacco and the Legend of the Pipe

In spite of all the warnings millions of dollars are spent annually on advertising alone by the tobacco industry.

Our ancestors must be appalled. This is one of the things Indians get blamed for, and of a truth, there are many of our people who have joined the club. But today's consumption of tobacco is a far cry indeed from the use to which it was put in the old days.

Tobacco smoldered and made smoke. Smoke rose and carried to heaven the incense of the cedar shavings with which it had been mixed. Today's various "blends" are a far cry from the old "Oh-yenh-gwah-onh-weh," the real tobacco.

Even during my generation, women going to the fields and forests to collect herbs took along a little bag of cedar shavings and tobacco, not to smoke but to toss upon a little fire as a thank offering for the medicine they were about to find.

The pipe was not brought forth from its beautifully decorated bag to share a smoke with just any casual visitor. It was reserved for the most solemn councils or held high in sacred ritual. It was the incense of the cedar shavings that was supposed to be pleasing to God. The tobacco merely kept the embers smoldering and produced the smoke on which it rose. The ritual of the peace pipe served the same purpose as offering an invocation at the start of an important meeting.

Pipes were made of various materials, but the original and best came from Pipestone, Montana. The legend of the coming of the peace pipe indicates that it was intended as a sort of portable altar.

All the nations of the earth were at war. The battle cries of the warriors echoed and reechoed on the winds. From sunrise to sunset the fighting continued and there were many days of fighting. The numbers of dead and wounded grew ever larger until even the stones of the battlefield were crimson.

All the nations of the land were fighting for power over one another. There was no thought or hope of peace. The law of the Great Spirit that there should be equality between man and man was forgotten.

In sorrow the Great Spirit gazed down upon his red children. He was distressed and weary with the constant din of battle. He had not placed the tribes of men on the earth to quarrel with one another. He wished his children to dwell in peace, for the land was vast and could be shared by all.

So he leaped upon a mountain peak above the place of battle and, in a great voice of thunder, called all the warring nations together in council. On the battleground with its crimson stones the gathering took place. This spot was designated ever after as neutral territory. The Great Spirit made of it a sacred place, sanctified by those who had given up their lives.

62

From the red stone the Great Spirit broke a piece and fashioned a pipe. He placed within the bowl the fragrant bark of the cedar and lit it with eternal fire. The smoke drifted into the sky and vanished, symbolizing from that day forth the mingling of man with the spirit of the Great Mystery.

The Old People were firmly convinced about the power of the pipe and fully aware that, as with anything else in the realm of medicine or the sacred mysteries, it was to be used only at certain times and with due observance of the ritual. It was part and parcel of their belief that such things misused could turn and destroy those who used them for evil purposes.

All who touched the pipe must be prepared to keep the pledge of peace, even at the risk of their lives, for it had been fashioned by the very hand of the Great One who had made them in the long ago.

There is a story that is told of a council between enemies, one very similar to the one at the time of the Peace Pipe gift, for there was much anger and each tribe was determined to be the victor over the other.

Three times the sacred pipe had passed around the circle and the bearers were met with sullen looks and downcast eyes. No warrior would touch the stem, for to touch it meant that a pact had been made.

On the fourth time around, a woman with a baby in her arms chanced to edge closer to the council ring. Laughing, the child reached out and grasped the pipe, and in shame the warriors followed so that peace was at once established and firmly kept.

CHAPTER 9

The Tradition of the Clans

Students of Indian history sooner or later become involved in the complicated riddle of tribes and subtribes. Of the hundreds of tribes named in the accounts of early explorers, many have become extinct. Disagreement in leadership sometimes divided a tribe; warfare and expediency sometimes merged tribes so that the origins of one or the other were lost. The original names were often unpronounceable for the white man who substituted his own meaningless terms.

For example, the original name for the Oneida tribe was *O-NA-YOTE-KA-O-NA.* This was quite a mouthful to pronounce; however, the word had a definite meaning— "The people of the Standing Stone." The name came from the legend of their long migration. It was said that at every place they settled there was an upright stone. When they found it necessary to move on, they would find the stone awaiting them at a newly designated homesite. (Perhaps if one searched long and diligently, the path of this people could be traced backward to a Central American beginning.)

In the city of Lancaster, Ohio, is the mighty bulk of

Mt. Pleasant thrusting into the sky. From the summit of its great cliff one can overlook miles of the surrounding territory. It would have been a position any tribe would covet. A woman whose family had lived in the area for generations remembers that her grandfather spoke of one particular spot on the mountain called "the Standing Stone," though there seems to be no such formation there at this time. It is quite likely that the ancestors of the Oneida spent some time in that area, for they have a tradition that they passed through the country of the mounds while the early inhabitants were still residing there.

Further investigation into the traditions of the Oneidas indicates that they were related by blood to many tribes. They are often called the little brothers of the Mohawks; in fact, the languages of the two tribes are so similar that they have little difficulty understanding each other. Aside from their undoubted common origin with others of the Iroquois Nation, they numbered among their cousins the Hurons, the Tionontati or Tobacco Nation, the Neutral Nation, the Nottaway, the Meherrin, the Munsies, the Wenro, and the Susquehannocks.

It is surprising to me that scholars who can reel off names of tribal groups like the ABCs pay so little attention to the clans into which the tribes are divided. In certain ways the clan is more important than the tribe. A traveling Indian may mention to another Indian the name of the tribe from which he comes. The information will be greeted with polite smiles and possibly a gracious inclination of the head in acknowledgment of the greatness of that nation. If, however, the traveler wears upon his garments the totem of his clan, someone may leap joyfully out of a crowd, clasp him in quick and eager kinship, and whisper, "Me, also."

Most tribes have special laws regarding marriage within the clan. One may marry within the tribe—but to marry within the clan would be to marry one's sister!

Not all tribes have the same number of clans; some have only three, others six or seven. Yet the clan totems are pretty much the same: the deer, wolf, bear, crane, beaver, turtle, and others jealously guard their totemic origins. Tribal custom dictates whether children enter the mother's clan or the father's but they usually remain in that group for life.

There are rare exceptions. I remember years ago there was a family of the Turtle Clan who had a young, much-loved son. The lad had been sickly from birth. In spite of a special diet, trips to the white doctor, and potions from the medicine man, he grew slowly and was weak and listless. Finally, the medicine man announced a startling diagnosis: the lad was "out of his clan." A great feast was arranged and the clans gathered to see who would claim him. The Bear Clan came forth. In rough and brawny arms they clasped him, tumbled him on the ground, cuffed him, and pushed him in ursine play. Weak and spindly as he was, he took no harm, but rolled and frolicked with the rest. That day he became a Bear and, strangely enough, immediately began to flourish. Straight, tall, and well-muscled he became—the boy who was born "out of his clan."

It is not difficult to theorize on the origins of tribal organizations. While the ancient Indian had unlimited personal freedom, experience had taught him that he fared better as part of a group. Scattered family groups were at the mercy of the wilderness and attackers. So they gathered together under a common leader. The stronger the leadership, the better for the tribe.

But why the clan?

There are legends without number of animals who talked, taught, and fathered certain nations. These legends serve their purpose. They make fine telling about the campfires but, more important, they keep alive particular virtues to be passed on to one's offspring—the industry of the beaver, the aloof dignity of the crane, the fleetness of the deer. They also open the ears to the voice of nature, whose creatures teach the arts of survival to him who is not too proud to learn.

But common sense indicates that there is something more back of it all.

In the jungles of Central America, a pile of rubble yielded to the spade; eventually there stood forth, if not in its original glory, a building of impressive dimensions. No airy, fairy palace this. It was foursquare and solid; stocky, sturdy, like a warrior stripped to the essentials for battle. A frieze of marching turtles decorated the cornice and from this the archaeologist gave the ancient building its modern name, the House of the Turtle. A bell of truth may have been rung at last.

An old tradition among North American Indians tells of a great migration of the Serpent People led by the Turtle. It was wise for the planners of the exodus to enlist as guides and protectors a powerful warrior band. It is said by the old people that having successfully made the circuit of the Great Gulf and having fought their way through untold wildernesses and savage conflict, they came at last into a place of pleasant valleys, peaceful streams, and tree-clad slopes. It was truly a land flowing with milk and honey. Here they paused long enough to build a mighty memorial to the Serpent led by the Turtle.

The effigy mound in southern Ohio has been variously described as a snake with an egg in its mouth, a symbol of creation, and nonsense too fantastic to repeat. Nowhere in Indian serpent legends could we find reference to an egg.

But a turtle. . . .

CHAPTER 10

The Migration of the Serpent People

It is said that in the very long ago, a people lived far to the south who were forced to flee from their powerful and cruel enemies. These people had many towns and villages and were very numerous, but they were a gentle people, and now the rulers had become corrupt and oppressive.

It is said that they went first to Turtle who was very wise in all the ancient knowledge. He agreed to lead them on their journey. Bear also accompanied them to protect them with his strength. Crane was of the party because of his knowledge of the water and Wolf was to scout and warn them of their enemies.

These people were of the Serpent Nation, and according to their custom they fasted, prayed, and performed certain rituals to prepare for their journey.

It is said they traveled a great water close to shore on their rafts. At last they landed and turned northward into the wilderness.

They traveled for many months and suffered much hunger. At last, Turtle in his wisdom spoke to them. "It is because we are so many that the game is fleeing before us, and we shall all die of hunger. Here we shall separate into smaller bands and each will take its own direction."

71

The people began to murmur and to grieve that they would never see their relatives again. Still, it was wisdom that they part company, so it was decided to build a great monument; in the years to come, perhaps their children would pass this way and remember a time when they were all brothers.

I will tell you how I first saw the Serpent Mound and what it meant to me. The legend of the migration of the Serpent People was one of many we had heard in our childhood and in our travels. As we found mounds and effigies there was always the hope that somewhere the great monument might exist. Oddly enough, we had read of the serpent mound in southern Ohio and had heard the various theories regarding the egg in its mouth. We were very perplexed about this; it had no meaning at all for us.

The serpent we could understand.

The Indian knows that there is no such thing as an "Indian race." We are several races, and not all of us came from the same place or at the same time. But there is one definite and definitive separation between those who came by water and those who came by land.

Those who came across the land bridge are Coyote; those who came by water are Serpent. It is very hard to put into English the meaning and power of those names. Though the two were bitter enemies, neither of the terms implied any disparagement of those who bore them.

To most Americans a coyote is something of a pest, skulking and sly. To an Indian he is a token of fleetness and stamina. He has the innate ability to organize pursuit or retreat.

72

A serpent is now the epitome of evil, the very personification of Satan himself. To our people he is the symbol of wisdom—and holy wisdom, at that.

So it was that I came blindly to my first visit to the Serpent Mound. It was a lovely Sunday morning. We were all in a very gay mood as we set out after church for a picnic lunch at the state park a short drive away.

We trooped across the beautiful lawns and climbed the visitor's tower. I looked at legend come alive, for there beneath me I saw not an egg (unless an egg has a head) but the turtle and the serpent. My eyes filled with tears and I wished—oh, how I wished—that Grey Owl were still with me.

My companions were full of questions and I pointed to the small triangular mound at the front of the "egg."

"That," I said, "is the head of a turtle. I am sure of it. I am Turtle and have many times woven the symbol of my clan in the beadwork for my family. The triangular head is the only possible way to make a turtle out of a simple oval."

We trooped down and into the museum, and there on the wall were drawings of the mound as it had looked originally.

There was the great serpent coiling sinuously. There in its wideflung jaws was the great oval-shaped mound with the small triangular shape at the front. But there were also long legs extending from the back of the oval and stretching beyond the jaws of the serpent. Now there could be no doubt.

The turtle sign is used almost universally among Indian tribes. It is a common name with a descriptive word: Little

Turtle, Sleeping Turtle, and so on. There are Turtle Clans in many tribes. The shape of the shell and the position of the limbs are used to denote descriptive terms. For instance an octagon shaped shell with all the legs withdrawn may indicate a sleeping turtle. The shell is variously depicted as oval, octagon, or occasionally even a square.

But if you want to say, "This turtle is traveling, going somewhere," there is only one way to do it—lengthen the back legs.

One of the elders of the church, working toward his master's degree at the university, was intrigued with this new explanation of the effigy and wanted to use it in a term paper. The only drawback was that he needed a reference. He finally suggested that somewhere there might be some old Indian who knew the beliefs of our people and who could be quoted as an authority.

I am afraid I laughed to suddenly realize that I am an old Indian, but I could speak only for my own beliefs. With much more enterprise than I would ever have had, this young man located an old Indian in Pennsylvania and wrote to him. He simply asked if there were anything the Indian could tell about the Serpent Mound in Ohio. When the reply came back, he brought the letter to me.

With wonder and excitement I read almost the same story I had told, except that the writer remembered going with his people to this place to dance at the great memorial, for it was holy ground.

Knowledge of our past increases year by year as we who were lost to each other become reunited. Will we, when all truth is revealed, sift fact from legend and know the origin of our clans, our fathers?

CHAPTER 11

The Prophet

Throughout our years together, it was occasionally necessary for Grey Owl to travel without the family. Sometimes the trips kept him from home for several weeks. The government had declared its willingness to settle Indian land claims, and there were many conferences to insure that all the papers were in order. Decisions needed to be made about what to do with the money, should it ever be forthcoming.

I was embarrassed one time when a neighbor said indignantly, "I think that's terrible! How can he leave you and all these children? What does he think you live on?"

In thinking it over, I was a bit surprised to find that I had never considered this side of it. Grey Owl was a good father, daily concerned for his children, sensitive to their moods and understanding their need for love. Actually, our little business proceeded just as well whether he was at home or away, but now I realized that, strangely enough, when I was alone all the handcraft orders fell within my capabilities.

When he returned I told him about the neighbor's thoughts. He was not greatly disturbed, but said white people had a different philosophy. He said that our tradition taught long ago that all children belong to the Supreme Being and are only loaned to us. Also that grown people are their guardians on earth and have to trust that the Father-of-all will provide the necessities of life.

He added that when he had to be absent he simply said, "Father, here are your children. I leave them in your care," and went in full confidence that they would be provided for as well or better than he could do himself.

This utter and complete trust in God is inherent in much of our philosophy and sometimes causes us to appear lacking in diligence.

There was an old man who lived on our reserve years ago. He had two unmarried daughters who kept his house as best they could but they were very poor. Only occasionally could he find work with a road crew or some harvest work for a farmer. He had a little garden, but the soil was poor and his crops were meager. Nevertheless, it was a firm household rule that all who came to visit should be fed.

One day several people had come to see him. The conversation was enjoyable and the day slipped swiftly by toward evening. He became more and more uneasy when his daughters failed to begin preparations for a meal and they avoided his eyes.

Finally he called them outside and said, "Daughters, these people are hungry and have a long way to go. You must fix some supper."

They replied that there was nothing in the house except a few potatoes and if they cooked these, he would have nothing to eat the next day.

"How can you have so little faith?" he cried. "Don't

you know that unless you share what you have to the last crumb, you will get no more? Cook the potatoes, and I'll guarantee there will be more when we need them."

The visitors ate and there was neither apology nor complaint about the meal. When they rose from the table, they thanked the women as sincerely as though it had been a feast.

During his travels, Grey Owl made many friends among the various tribes, and they often sat for hours comparing legends and traditions as well as their present-day problems.

He noticed that although nature legends often differed, and historical tradition told of different experiences, all the tribes shared one common memory—that of a wonderful prophet and teacher, a holy man who walked among the people in ages long gone by. Though he was called by various names and the stories differed from tribe to tribe, all agreed upon this point: the Divine Visitor was pale of skin, had sea-green eyes, and a beard and hair of copper color.

Always he taught the lessons of love and peace, of man's obligation to his fellowman, and of the love of the Father-of-all for his children. It was he who had instituted all our finer impulses of concern for one another.

I loved to hear Grey Owl repeat the stories he had heard, and it was not until several years after his death that I found them once again in a beautiful book, *He Walked the Americas,* by L. Taylor Hansen (Amherst Press, 1963).

It is not necessary to repeat Mr. Hansen's legends; however, Grey Owl had another to add.

It is said that once very long ago before the coming of the white man, long before the time of our grandfather's grandfathers, a stranger came to our people.

He appeared suddenly, as they were gathered together about the council fire; and at first the people were much afraid, thinking him to be a spirit. It is said that he was of strange appearance, that his skin was pale as a ghost, and there was hair upon his face.

But soon they saw that they had nothing to fear, for he said that he had come from the Great Spirit to teach them to live in love together.

Food was brought to him, and as he ate he told many stories of a land far away across the water where people had become very wicked. He said he had many enemies but the worst of these was the Spirit of Evil who led men astray and caused them to hate each other.

It is said he taught many things about medicine and healing and repeated to them many rituals.

At last one of the people asked by what name he might be called and he answered that wherever he traveled, men gave him a name according to their language. At this, the people told him, "It is our custom to use the names given to us in our childhood." They would prefer to use the name by which he was known in his own country.

And the name he left with them was Yé-Sos—Yé-Sos Gah-lis-tos.

Quetzalcoatl is sometimes called the Divine Lord of the People of the South. There are many books written about him. Historians are skeptical of his antiquity and disagree about his origins, but the attributes of Quetzalcoatl and the belief of his followers is recognizable to the

Northern Indian. He was also known as Kukulcan and Viracocha.

A very long time ago, Quetzalcoatl descended from the sky where he had been God of the Air. He became as man and lived among them. It was said that he had been born of a virgin in a far country and had been killed upon a tree by his enemies. Then he came to the Beautiful People in his original godly form.

He taught the people to come joyously to the temple with gifts of fruit and flowers. He taught the obligation of man to God, of parents to children, and of all to the aged. His symbol was the feathered serpent because he had power over both Wind and Water.

He left them at last with a promise to return and bring a time of great peace and renewal.

As time went on the people he had taught were conquered by first one enemy and then another. Those who were left alive began to lose faith and despaired of seeing him again.

Then out of the North came a nation more cruel and powerful than any other, and as other conquerors have done before and since, they allowed the people to remember the name of their God in feasts and festivals. But his symbol, the Feathered Serpent, was set up as a terrible god who demanded human sacrifice.

Not long before Columbus, there lived in this land a great king named Nezahualcóyotl. During his youth, he had been forced to flee those powerful chiefs who envied his inheritance and during this time he lived among the common people who learned to love him. When at last he became king, he made many good laws to relieve their condition, and he tried to stop the constant round of human sacrifice. He built a great and beautiful temple with a great tower whose roof was painted black and gilded with stars.

This was the temple of the Cause of all Causes, the unnameable God, and no image was allowed within. Only flowers and secret gums were brought here as sacrifices.

When his grandson Ixtlilxóchitl was born, the astrologers advised him to destroy the child because if he lived, it would be his destiny to unite with his enemies and betray their country.

However, Nezahualcóyotl was convinced that the return of Quetzalcoatl was near and thought this was what the astrologers referred to. When the Spanish came, all thought their bearded white gods had returned in the ships and the grandson of the Good King joined with Cortez in the overthrow of their civilization.

CHAPTER 12

The Mounds

We came to Ohio in a blue and gold October nearly twenty years ago. People have often asked why we chose to remain in this area so far from our reservation. We might answer that here we found the kindest neighbors, a warm reception—and that would be true. Or we might say there seemed to be a demand for our handcrafts, and that also would be true.

Actually, in spite of the acceptance by the community, we were very lonely for our own friends and relatives. And to tell the truth, we were a bit overwhelmed. Miles upon hundreds of miles of farms and villages and cities filled with white people. Not an Indian anywhere. We were a tiny island in the midst of the sea.

But here, surrounding the town of Newark, were many places dear to Indian memory. Flint Ridge is nearby. Our ancestors came each year in the old days to get material for arrowheads, spearpoints, and knives. Here were the old trails that had known the moccasined feet of Delaware, Shawnee, Miami, Wyandotte, and many others.

Here also were the giant earthworks of the Old People. Before the town was built, the earthen walls rose everywhere for miles. Great passageways connected many of the enclosures. Now, highways, railroads, and cities have demolished most of these. Only a few remain, beautifully preserved by the State Historical Society.

The Octagon Mound encloses fifty acres and adjoins by a short passage a circle thirty acres in extent.

Another, just at the outskirts of the town, is a great circular earthwork with an effigy called an Eagle in the center. The gate to this is seventy-five feet wide and the walls rise about ten to fifteen feet as viewed from the deep moat inside.

The people responsible for all this earth moving are called Mound Builders, an obvious term but one which leaves the impression that they were a separate race of people, long extinct before the "Indian race" came into existence. Some historians are a bit smug about it and insist the Indian knew nothing about the mounds except that they were built by the "Old People."

Such an opinion serves only to illustrate the well-known communication gap. To us the words "Old People" is a very expressive term. It means ancestors so far removed that only a shadow of memory remains, a memory of people who were wiser than we. The Indian recognized no peers among his contemporaries. He knew all he needed to know about the land upon which he lived. Efficient in hunting, brave in war, learned in the products of field and woodland—these he had to be to survive. But he was fully aware of his ancestors, the Old People, who had lived a different kind of life somehow and were very wise.

The very morning after our arrival, we headed for

Mound Builders Park, location of the great circle mound with the Eagle inside. We went there as one would go to Arlington National Cemetery, with the same heavy feeling of sadness. Here were the graves of ancient holy men, but beyond that, the earthwork enclosed ground so sacred we hesitated to set our feet upon it.

We climbed to the top of the wall and looked down into the moat inside and across the flat, clipped grass. Grey Owl was explaining that at one time there had been a palisade of logs where we were standing. A man nearby said, "Strangers here? What do you think of it?"

"They surely keep it nice," said Grey Owl, "That's really . . ."

"Huh! This is nothing," the man retorted. "Used to have the fairgrounds out here and this was sure one fine racetrack."

A little sick, we began to turn away when some devil of perversity made Grey Owl ask, "What happened to the cross?"

"What cross?"

"There was supposed to be a cross in the middle."

"Oh, that's no cross," said the man. "That's an eagle over there. Come on, I'll show you."

In an embarrassed silence we followed him across the wide lawn to an elevation in the center. Our guide scrambled up the sloping mound. Back and forth he stomped, waving his arms to show us the wings. We stood on the level ground and waited.

"Come on up," the man shouted. "You can see all around from here."

Grey Owl turned swiftly and strode away. I murmured a weak "thank you" over my shoulder.

"It *was* a cross," Grey Owl insisted as he paced the floor that night. "It was a cross. I saw the map—old—painted on hide. Everything else is there. But it was a cross!"

I had never seen him so disturbed.

At the time of this encounter with the stranger at the mound, we were visiting in the home of a friend whose family had been in Newark almost from its beginning. In answer to our questions, she remembered her grandfather telling that digging had been done in several places. But it was many months and many books later that the pattern began to emerge. At last our search was rewarded. There had been an excavation "to the center."

We forgave the Historical Society who really did a beautiful job, all things considered.

The following might be considered a little history lesson:

The first settlement in Newark was a colony of some twenty hardy souls headed by Elias Hughes and John Radcliff in 1798. Before then, in the ten years following the opening of the Ohio territory, surveyors, traders, and explorers moved through in search of choice locations. It is recorded that Christopher Gist passed through the area in 1751 and the Reverend David Jones in 1773.

The discovery of the mounds is credited to Isaac Stadden in 1800, though how these other people could travel the area and avoid the interminable system of causeways and earthworks is hard to imagine.

Timothy Jenkins, writing in 1893, said that he had

been familiar with the circle mound for more than fifty-five years. He had hunted there as a young man when it was covered with gigantic trees and tangled underbrush. By 1896, when Howe wrote his *Historical Collections of Ohio,* he described the effigy as an eagle.

Several excavations were attempted in the intervening years, but nothing "of value" was found—just some charcoal and pieces of bone—so it was abandoned.

The fever to dig in the mounds persists even today. People still insist "there's gold in them thar hills." Today, flints and other relics have an intrinsic value, but in the early days they were mere curiosities. People were looking for gold. Countless sites were torn into with the spade, the dirt thrown aside, and finally the whole thing given up in disgust.

Today, when we speak of an excavation to the center, we think of a shaft sunk through successive layers. To people who were only looking for treasure, it very likely meant something else.

Imagine we are the diggers. Suppose we begin with a four-armed cross. Shovels flying, we dig into one of the slightly higher elevations of the mound with, of course, more energy than caution. Nothing here, dig farther. At last we come to those few old bones. Disgusting! Must have burnt their captives here. Remember at this point we're not trying to restore; we are only digging. We pick up our shovels and walk away, leaving the dirt scattered where it fell.

Later another comes. "There must be some treasure here. Try this side."

So what is left when the Historical Society begins the

restoration is the three armed figure, the lateral parts tipped slightly like an eagle's wings.

Well, it's only theory, I'll admit. All I know is, at the time of the vernal equinox, the rising sun shoots its golden arrow straight through the great gateway to the temple mound.

All I know is that there is now no place for the chief holy man to stand for the ritual. He cannot stand where the "head" is said to be. To do so would be to trample on the grave of one of the greatest of the ancients.

All I know is that the place is very sacred, and very beautiful—and very sad.

CHAPTER 13

The Ghost Dance Religion

Indians accept dreams, prophecies, and revelation as facts of life. Students of "Indian lore" are not unduly impressed, claiming that most primitive societies are credulous of these mysteries.

However, the particular subject matter of some of the dreams and prophecies must give us pause.

Consider the Ghost Dance religion.

Its prophet and founder was a Paiute, the humble son of a former Paiute holy man. He had no education and certainly had given no evidence in his earlier life that he would ever be anything more than what he was, a ranch hand for a white settler. He knew a smattering of English but no other Indian language. Yet within a few months, Indians from all over the country were to come at the risk of their lives to his home in the mountains of Nevada.

His name was Wovoka and this was the way it began.

In 1889 Wovoka, the Paiute, fell desperately ill and on the day of the total eclipse of the sun, he lapsed into unconsciousness. In view of his illness, it seemed to be a coma preceding death. It was quite unexpected, then, when he awoke refreshed and began to relate a dream he had had during the period of his unconsciousness.

His soul had traveled to the borders of the world and there he saw all the people who had died long ago, all happy and young, engaged in their old-time occupations. He talked also with a bright and shining being whom he assumed to be God. He was told that it was not yet time for him to die; that he must go back and tell the Indians to be good and love one another, to live at peace with the white man and fight no more wars. There was no promise that the Indian would regain his own, but in heaven he would have again all that he had lost.

Officials and reporters of that day found it hard to understand how this vision affected Indians in far-flung places, not knowing that it called to mind ancient prophecies half-forgotten in their misery and despair.

How they escaped the watchful eyes of the reservation superintendent and eluded the pony soldiers, how they survived the rigors of the long marches to the borders of Nevada no one ever will know; yet come they did to tell their stories of starvation and misery to this man with a dream. Their desperate plight moved him, and his prophecy expanded. Not only in heaven but on earth, the millennium would come. There would be earthquakes and upheaval and their dead would rise. Fathers and mothers would be reunited with children; friends and lovers would meet once more. And out of a cloud would come the Rejuvenator. He would come once more to men as He had promised.

The old and weary earth would be rejuvenated and all men would be reborn. The white man would inherit a world suitable for him and the Indian would be reborn into his own, and heaven and earth would be in harmony again. Peace was the core of the religion. Be still, Indians; love God and each other. He can do His own work in His season and it will soon be over. Meanwhile a new dance was instituted with special garments commemorating the promise, with the secret sacred crosses upon the breast.

To the white men it was just another religion and religion made the Indian wild. The only dances the soldiers recognized were war dances—and besides, there was that Custer affair.

At Wounded Knee on December 29, 1890, just about a year after its birth in the dream of an Indian ranch hand, the Ghost Dance religion went down in a field of blood.

On that day some three hundred converts to the religion of Wovoka gathered to participate in the Ghost Dance. In among the people rode the pony soldiers and confiscated all the arms and ammunition. Ninety-six men and two hundred women and children were shot down without mercy.

The crosses on the Ghost Dance shirts shone wetly under the snow.

CHAPTER 14

The Code of Handsome Lake

Handsome Lake 1735-1815, b. Seneca Village Conewages on the Genessee r. Half brother of Cornplanter. Founder and teacher of Gai-wiio, the "new religion" of the Iroquois.

Cold words to describe the man whose influence on Indian thought continues still. What was it with these prophets? Almost without exception ordinary men, some of them with more vices than virtues, suddenly they were touched with fire.

Is it that a man sees best the stars when he is prone? Perhaps, for they all seem to have known a common affliction—deep despair, blindness, or serious illness that gave them time to reflect.

There have been philosophies expressed in fancier language, but few which enumerated so clearly the sins of modern man as does Handsome Lake's Gai-wiio, the "new" religion.

He ought not to be remembered for the first part of his life, when he was just another drunken Indian carousing his life away. Even then, he must have possessed a certain sweetness of character since we know that his daughter and her husband nursed him tenderly in his almost fatal illness.

And then he dreamed his dream. In another time, among another people, it would have been called a vision or a revelation. Indians have dreams.

No matter. He met in his dream three messengers (later they were joined by a fourth) who said they were ordained by the Creator to appear to men at certain times of need to offer aid and to teach again the laws by which men ought to live.

The Code of Handsome Lake, resulting from the contact with these heavenly visitors, is outlined in a series of sermonettes that have become ritual to his followers. The exact translation and form of ritual, I believe, should concern only those who still practice it. The principles set forth might apply to all of us.

The first four rules of the Code admonish against drinking, charms and witchcraft, abortion, and desertion of a family, in that order. Considering that we all seem to learn the vices of civilization much faster than we learn the virtues, three of those were vital in the hoped-for reclamation of his people.

It was in the second that Handsome Lake clashed with the "old" religion. There had come to be a concentration of effort on medicine, a forgetting that the true old wisdom said that spells and charms were most dangerous to those who wrought them. The Old People taught that, although there is such a thing as the arcane knowledge of the forces of nature and that many of her products could kill as well as cure, such knowledge was *not* to be used by amateurs nor for evil purposes.

Others of the principles set forth are very modern in tone. Consider the one that admonishes parents to rear their children well, to love them and to discipline them with understanding patience.

But I wonder what some of the modern cultists who think being Indian meant the permissiveness to "do your own thing" would think of the laws governing the marriage code.

There were regular marriage customs. Incidentally, mothers-in-law were not to spread dissent. Neither a husband or wife was to strike one another. Here was inserted the Indian version of the Golden Rule which was much older than Handsome Lake: "Even as you desire good treatment, so render it."

Many of Handsome Lake's teachings were given in parables. In one, we learn that mutual trust and faithfulness in marriage is essentially important.

The "now" generation would be impressed with the admonition to parents that they ought to listen to the good advice from their children and refrain from belittling them.

As for good community relations, it fell upon each individual to feed the poor, adopt the orphans, care for and respect the aged.

Gossiping, talebearing, boasting, and vanity were mortal sins—and those who listened to such things were equally guilty. Handsome Lake's advice to his people to farm, to build good houses, and to seek education was followed by a warning that they were not to be lifted up in pride of these possessions.

They were to learn the language and the ways of the

white man and to adopt such improvements as would be of lasting benefit to the people.

Do these precepts sound familiar? It seems to me that the message of ideal moral law has been given over and over to men in many lands and conditions. Is it so strange to believe that a merciful God could have spoken once more, to a people overwhelmed by despair and losing touch with the last dim memory of a purer faith?

Consider Handsome Lake's vision of Segan'-hedŭs, He Who Resurrects. It is to be found in Section 84 of the Great Message during the episode of the Journey Over the Great Sky-road.

The four messengers had conducted the prophet through a series of visions and now they passed a man who paused to ask a question of him.

"Did you never hear your grandfathers say that once there was a certain man upon the earth across the great waters who was slain by his own people?"

The prophet answered that yes, he had heard this story from his "Grandparents."

"I am he," proclaimed the stranger, "Segan'-hedŭs—He Who Resurrects."

He then showed his hands and feet scarred with old wounds and his breast pierced by a spear.

Said the man, "They slew me because of their independence and unbelief. So I have gone home to shut the doors of Heaven that they may not see me again until the earth passes away."

Segan'-hedŭs then asked how the people seemed to be receiving the new teachings. Upon hearing that perhaps half of them were inclined to believe the prophet, he said with some bitterness, "You are more successful than I, for some believe in you, but none in me." (Translation of the Gai-wiio by William Bluesky, lay preacher of the Baptist Church.)

It would be perfectly natural to assume that Handsome Lake had received the story of a Savior from his Christian neighbors and included it in his Code as one of the beliefs of the white man that might benefit his people.

There is, however, little evidence that he was impressed with Christianity, the white man's religion. It is more apparent that he was attempting to revitalize the old moral law from which he felt his people had departed in their contact with civilization.

And though it is said that he received some instruction from his nephew Henry Obail (Abeal), his admission that he had heard the story of Segan'-hedŭs from his "Grand-parents" means to an Indian something quite apart from its significance in modern English. It means something handed down, passed on from ancient times.

Grey Owl once said that Christianity had little impact upon his people until they learned to read. When they read the first five books of the Bible, they said, "Why, this is not the white man's religion; it is our old time belief."

Brothers! In your recitals of the Gai-wiio, bear in mind the memories of your Grandparents, the Ancient Ones.

CHAPTER 15

Invitation to Scholars

I have never been one to engage in idle, wishful thinking. Indeed, life has been so full there has been little time for that. To raise the children of Grey Owl and raise them well, to fully enjoy them as they grew, and to share over the teacups their adventures now that they are grown—as the poet says, "that were heaven enough."

And then, in this small corner of the Beloved Land, there is such a wealth of adventure in the past. In one small library there are racks of old books one couldn't read in a lifetime.

Still—now that the toys are put away, the everlasting search for missing socks is over, and the last of the baseball gloves is stored in the attic awaiting the grandchildren— now there is time for dreaming.

There are times when I long for my beloved. And for a moment I wish we were just beginning our search; that we had time and a magic carpet to go where the adventure of learning called.

We would stand on the ancient battleground at Spiro, Oklahoma, where two cultures met in fatal combat. We would stand and defend it against the idle curious, the treasure seekers, for the treasure that is there is for the scholars.

We would journey to Etowah, Georgia, the land of the Sun Chiefs. In imagination we would see them in their glory, borne high on the shoulders of their people, the fading memory of their fathers the Sun Kings flaring for a crystal moment as their feathers turned to gold in a setting sun.

We would seek the lost and sacred city at the Cross of Waters—so dimly remembered it is but a legend.

Knowledge, like gold, is where you find it. To dare to search where men have not searched before is high adventure. To find your answers in the most unlikely places is the ultimate in satisfaction.

But to reach an impasse in your search and then suddenly find your shovel filled with treasure lifts you to the clouds.

Many of the books we longed to see in our search for the ancients were out of print and the few copies in existence closely guarded.

In vain we sought the *Traditions of Dee-Coo-Dah.*

There were vague references to it in many later manuscripts, but it seemed to be lost forever to the general public. The story of how it came to be written was so typical of the attitudes of our people that it seemed to us it must be true and could answer many of our questions.

In the days when the first settlers moved into the midwest, there were mounds and earthworks in every state east of the Mississippi. Digging in the mounds became a favorite pastime and little by little they were being demolished.

A young Virginian traveling through the territory was disturbed by this and began to make diagrams of all the mound complexes he could find. In the course of his travels he met an old Indian who was intrigued with the novelty of a white man who did not come to destroy but to observe.

At last they began to talk, cautiously at first. The old man was curious; why did his friend not come to dig when he was obviously interested? The young man really did not know, except that it seemed wrong, somehow.

I can picture in my mind how the old man watched from lowered eyes for any sign of false interest. How many times he would begin to speak and then fall silent. How he would reveal a glimpse of his story and wait to see if the young man would receive. And then at last, his confidence fully established, his joy that here was one to whom he could pass tradition before he died; a man of a different race, but perhaps that was part of the plan—there was no one else.

So when the young man presented his diagrams and maps, his Indian friend would identify them and tell about the people responsible for their building.

How we longed to see this book. Here perhaps was the link we were sure existed between the people of the North and those of the South.

It took eighteen years to get to the Library of Congress. I approached it in trepidation; how could I believe that even I could see and touch the treasury of books? But suddenly, at my request, there was the book I had waited for so long—the *Traditions of Dee-Coo-Dah.*

The young author's name was William Pigeon and from his book I learned at last why our people have a reverent awe for the earthworks at Newark, Ohio.

He described in detail the entire complex which occupied an "area of nearly two miles square." It consisted of three principal divisions—the Octagon, the Circle, and a square. These were connected by parallel walls and smaller works.

Of the entire complex it was the great circular earthwork that most impressed Willian Pigeon.

"In entering this ancient avenue for the first time, the visitor cannot fail to experience a sensation of awe such as he might feel in passing the portals of an Egyptian temple.

"In the center of the circle, there is a large embankment or rather a union of four mounds forming an unbroken outline."

I turned the page and there was the original map showing the four-armed cross within the circle.

When William Pigeon submitted his diagram of this complex to his friend Dee-Coo-Dah, the old man recognized it as the City of the Prophet. The entire works had been a "large metropolis or holy seminary of priests." The great circle mound was so sacred that only the priests and Holy Men were permitted inside the enclosure for the solemn religious observances.

I understood Grey Owl's rage and my own uneasiness at the desecration of this holy place.

I learned, too, that William Pigeon, though by his own admission the friend and adopted son of old Dee-Coo-Dah, was not above the desecration of the holy places when his friend was not around to see.

Did he feel shame the day he showed Dee-Coo-Dah the

diagrams of the Temple of Peace at Circleville, Ohio? Said the "illiterate savage,"

> "Seventy-six winters have passed away since last I visited that place where the bones of my fathers lie; and well do I remember that the oldest of my tribe boasted that the blood of man or beast never stained the earth within that circle."—*The Traditions of Dee-Coo-Dah,* p. 99.

All are gone, Dee-Coo-Dah—the sacred circle, and the temple mound, the village walls; and now you know the answer to your question flung in quick suspicious grief: "Do the bones of my fathers rest in peace?"

Scholar! Do you dare to be different? In all your studies of the origin of the Indian you have encountered many theories and each seemed more logical than the last. You've read that we came from Siberia, from Atlantis, from a lost continent in the Pacific; or that we were here from the dawn of time. One can find evidence of landings of Phoenician sailors, of the Romans, and many other people, but there is one theory that is seldom approached except in jest. That is the persistent possibility that the Indians may be descendants of the House of Israel.

But to prove or disprove any theory there must be investigation by many scholars. Relics, inscriptions, and graves must be examined, interpreted, and catalogued. This has to be done by men not only qualified to express an opinion but open-minded enough to accept evidence on its own merits, regardless of generally accepted ideas.

In reaching for the hidden past, the seeker may not

alone find his own cherished theories wrong; he may find another man's belief uncomfortably true. It will take more than cold research; it will require the hearts and understanding of people with great humility.

In a recent news item it was reported that a stone found in Tennessee in 1885 may be the cause of a complete reevaluation of other relics.

At first glance the stone didn't seem to offer much—a few scratched symbols; they had been found before and had been shoved aside as "coincidence" or "fake." Why was this different? Because for one of the first times a Hebrew-inscribed relic was unearthed under the direction of archaeologists working under ideal professional conditions.

But for an error of printing, it might have been deciphered long ago. The photograph of the stone, published by the Smithsonian Institution, was accidentally printed upside down. Its significance went unnoticed until it came to the attention of Dr. Joseph D. Mahau, Jr., of the Columbus, Georgia, Museum of Arts and Crafts.

He appealed to Cyrus H. Gordon, professor of Mediterranean Studies at Brandeis College, for an opinion on the stone.

Turned right side up, the inscription presented no problem. It translated from Hebrew: "For the land of Judah. . . ."

And the good professor advocated a reassessment of other relics.

By all means let us have a reassessment. Let us have all the relics out of their corners. Let us have the old diaries and letters of people who were in a position to observe the

Indian when he had only his own culture pattern by which to live.

Let us have the evidence of the Indian himself. Let us try a startling new method of investigation. Instead of formulating an opinion and *telling* the Indian what was history, let us ask him—with honest sincerity and even a certain humility—and be prepared to accept the truth even if it upsets our theories of migrations.

CHAPTER 16

The Case for Israel

The premise that the American Indian was descended from the lost tribes of Israel is greeted with derision by many historians. A writer often takes his reputation in his hands even to hint at it.

Indian children of the last few generations, learning their lessons from the same books used in the public schools, were taught the theory about migrations across the Bering Straits. Many Indians who do believe themselves children of the covenant are very careful to whom they talk about it.

It is comforting to believe that man has never fallen; that his rise from the slime of pre-history has been one long unbroken climb, and that there is no limit to which he cannot go. Still, we know this has not been true, at least in his past. As for the future, that remains to be seen.

Throughout the world are scattered remains of great cultures, mighty empires ruined and lost. "Asmodias, king of kings" is a shattered statue trampled by the plodding and unknowing feet of his descendants.

One thing that brought about the unpopularity of the Israel theory is that people tried too hard. They were looking for the lost "Ten Tribes" and they were trying to fit all Indians into that framework. Scholars can make a very good case for the Phoenicians, the Romans, and even the Welsh. It is fairly well established that the Chinese made at least one expedition in ancient times, not to mention the legends of the sky people or the undeniable presence of a prehistoric culture.

And then, of course, there is that convenient land bridge in the North. I read recently that there is now a school of thought which suggests that while people did cross by that route they were probably not the Indian as we know him today but a pre-dawn race. They need not have bothered. Until very recent dates, Eskimos were still traveling back and forth across the Bering Straits, having relatives on both sides.

That at least some Indians were descended from some of Israel seems undeniable in the face of evidence. Enough has already been found which if gathered and reevaluated would prove the point beyond the shadow of doubt.

Early writers who had access to Indian custom before the wind of "progress" blew away some of his beliefs have fallen into disrepute, and often their books are out of print, their names all but forgotten.

Relics supposed to have Hebrew inscriptions have disappeared into private collections or have been relegated to subterranean chambers of museums.

Many people have their personal theories and hope to have them vindicated. Grey Owl had a way of weeding out those whose interest was superficial.

We had been to town for groceries. Upon our return, we found a young man sitting in our yard. He jumped to his feet eagerly and cried, "Oh, I'm so glad to see an Indian here. I've been a student of Indian lore since I was just a boy, and at last there is someone to answer my questions."

His excitement shone in his face and Grey Owl handed me our packages and said, "I'll talk to this young man."

I knew because of the sincere interest of the stranger that nothing would be withheld. As I turned away, the youth said eagerly, "The first thing, Chief, do you have any idea where your people came from?"

For a moment we both froze. Then cautiously Grey Owl said, "Yes, I know. But can you take the truth if you hear it?"

His words stumbling with eagerness, the youth cried, "You know? You really know? I always thought you did. I mean, that Indians did—but they say—oh, tell me!"

"My people came from Israel," Grey Owl said quietly.

There was a moment's silence and the young man turned sadly away. "Oh, yes," he said, "I've heard that theory. But the books say your people came across the Bering Straits."

"That's what the books say?" said Grey Owl. "Then why come to me? Go back to your books, young man; they will answer your questions."

If he had been willing to listen, the youth would have heard the rest of it; that some people did indeed come across the Bering Straits; that we do not claim to be all the much sought long lost Ten Tribes.

Grey Owl said, "my people." He meant "my kind of Indian, my race." There are descendants of several races here. And when in the fullness of time all the truth is known, traces of many ancient wanderers will be found here in this fair land.

CHAPTER 17

The Sacred Name

One swallow doesn't make a summer, and a few words from a language don't prove a case. Language changes, but the last words to alter are those pertaining to religion or to the basic things of life.

Adair devoted thirty-six pages in his "Arguments" to a comparison of Indian and Hebrew language. He admitted that his knowledge of Hebrew was superficial, but he was impressed with the numerous words with identical or similar meanings in both languages. He dwelt at length upon the phonetics of the two and the peculiar idioms that seemed to him to denote an ancient relationship.

Here follow some examples:

English	Mohegan	Hebrew
I	Niah	Ani, or Ahni
Thou, thee	Keah	Ka
This man	Uwoh	Huah
We	Necaunuh	Nachnu

English	Creek	Hebrew
The first great cause	Ye hewah	Jehova
Praise the first great cause	Halleluwah	Hallelujah

English	Creek	Hebrew
Father	*Abba*	*Abba*
Now, the present time	*Na*	*Na*
Very hot, or bitter upon me	*Heru, hara, or hala*	*Hara hara*
To pray	*Phale*	*Phalac*
The hind parts	*Kesh*	*Kish*
One who kills another	*Abe* (derived from Abele Gruf)	*Abel*
War name who kills a rambling enemy	*Noabe,* compound of Noah and Abe	
Canaan	*Kenaai*	*Canaan*
Wife	*Awah*	*Eve or Eweh*
Winter	*Kora*	*Cora*
Another name for God	*Ale*	*Ale* or *Alohim*
Do	*Iennois*	*Iannon*

English	Penobscot	Hebrew
Arrarat, a high mountain	*Arrarat,* a high mountain	*Arrarat,* a high mountain

—Jenkins, pp. 73-75.

Here it may be well to interpose a word of caution, lest we take ourselves too seriously in a comparison of such fragments of languages. Historians may be forgiven for deriding the whole subject when unprofessional people begin to dabble in a science so exact.

Adair made at least one mistake very common among those unfamiliar with the interplay of language. He stated that the tribal name "Mohawk" was very apt for the "keepers of the law" among the Iroquois, since the word "Mhkohek" meant "law giver" in Hebrew. However, this name was not the original name of that tribe. They were so designated by their enemies, the Hurons, in whose language the word meant "eaters of men." One would have to go very far out on a limb to make a connection.

Still, it would seem that a comparative and comprehensive study would be interesting—though doubly difficult at this late time.

The universal law among Indians seems to have been that the name of God was too holy to be spoken in conversation so they devised or inherited many names which were actually the attributes of the Great Creator. For instance, among the Creeks, *Ishtohoollo* was the name for God to be used in conversation. It translated thus:

Ishto: great *Hoollo:* Sanctifying, sanctified, divine, or holy. To distinguish the divine name more strongly, they added:

Aba—father, *Ishtohoollo Aba*

Adair illustrated his point by describing a solemn ritual in which the divine name was intoned as a chant for a ceremonial dance. Even here, the name was not pro-

111

nounced in its entirety, but employed one syllable at a time in four separate dance cycles. Thus:

Chant for first dance phase: Y'ah- Y'ah- Y'ah- Y'ah-
Second phase: O- O- O- O-
Third phase: He- He- He- He-
Fourth phase: Wah- Wah- Wah- Wah—

The notes together compose their sacred, mysterious name, *Y-O-He-Wah.*

Add to this the description of the ancient sacred council circle and compare with Ezekiel's vision of the Cherubim (Ezekiel 1:10, 11).

In the sacred council were two white painted eagles with wings upspread and raised five feet from the ground close to the council seat. On the inner side of the notched pieces that hold up the eagles was painted with white clay the figure of a man with buffalo horns and a panther. These figures were painted afresh for the first fruits offering or annual atonement.

It is known to all these are not objects of worship as an Indian will hunt the eagle, the buffalo, or the panther. They are regarded as totems of the Great Spirit. Here in the circle they dance always in a bowing posture, frequently singing:

Al-le-wuh-wah
Yah-he-wah.

In his annual report in 1634, Father Paul le Jeune described a ceremony of the Montagnais, an Algonquian tribe. The ritual consisted of over four hours of continuous song. When he asked what the words meant, the celebrants were unable to tell him. Thus had the chants come down to them. The meaning was lost. Among most early accounts there are veiled hints of an ancient and separate language used only in traditional ritual.

Scattered throughout the land were certain towns designated as places of refuge to which criminals or even captives might flee and be safe from attack. Usually after a time, when tempers cooled, it was possible to secure the release of the offenders either through gifts to the families of those he had injured or through the intervention of holy men. There are stories, however, of some who spent their entire lives in these places which were in no sense prisons.

Appaliuchie-town of the Creek nation, esteemed as the mother town, was sacred to peace. No captives were put to death, no human blood spilt there.

Choate was situated on a large tributary of the Mississippi five miles above where *Fort-Loudon* once stood. Here in the latter part of the 1800's an Englishman claimed sanctuary after killing an Indian. He stayed there about three years until he had satisfied the friends of the deceased with gifts.

Koosah, a very old town still in existence in 1800, was used as a refuge for those who killed undesignedly.

It may be well to explain why so much more information has been cited about the Creek nation to the exclusion of other tribes who also have much to contribute to the subject.

To the Indian, his religious observances and traditions have been held sacred and inviolate. To many of them these seem "all we have left."

When one realizes that until farms and highways swept many of them away, there was a signal mound every seven to nine miles the length and breadth of the country, it becomes easier to comprehend that the Indian had firsthand and bitter knowledge of the Spanish occupation of Mexico. Add to that the eyewitness accounts of refugees fleeing from the oppression of those days and perhaps it will be plain that our ancestors knew of the wholesale slaughter and the burning of sacred literature. Despite the communication links it paid to appear ignorant over the years. Most of us have assumed that we had kept our most sacred rituals from public view.

The Creeks, however, from the earliest contact had friendly relations with the white man, due to trade. A few of those they had learned to trust were accepted into their councils, and some of these returned to write their observations.

It is not to conceal truth that I concentrate on simply gathering together those things that have already been written but to allow the tribes in the fullness of time to offer their own testimony—not for their own glory nor for that of any historian but to show the wisdom and mercy of the Supreme Being.

Dupratz, who also wrote *A Nation on the Mississippi,* reveals another sacred name.

He says they worshiped a Supreme Being called *Coyo-Cop-Chil.* The word *chil* signifies the highest degree of perfection.

Example: *oua*—fire

oua chil—supreme fire or sun

Coyo-Cop-Chil was so great and powerful that in comparison with him all things were nothing. He made all things—both those we can see and those unseen. He formed man with His own hands. He made him of clay and

114

finding it well-formed, He blew on his work and man began to live.

Adair reported that in all his forty years of experience with Indians from Hudson's Bay to the Mississippi, he never knew any of them to form any image of the Great Spirit they devoutly worshiped.

CHAPTER 18

Relics and Inscriptions

It was 1815 and farmer Marrick was plowing his fields. A low mound offered no obstacle to his plodding team. Up and over they went and his sharp eyes caught a glimpse of a strange "something" turned up by the plowshare.

He stopped his team and, wrapping the reins about the handle, stooped to pick up what appeared to be a bar about six inches long. At either end there was a loop. Upon closer examination he found the "bar" to be two pieces of rawhide sewed tightly together with sinew.

He tucked it into the band of his trousers and went on with his work. That evening he wiped the dirt from the surface and proceeded to clip the sinew. What he found between those old pieces of rawhide must have taxed his powers of understanding. Tightly creased and folded small were what appeared to be four pieces of parchment. Working with patience, he managed to unfold them and found them covered with some strange form of writing.

Later, a neighbor accidentally tore one piece to shreds as he examined it. According to the account of the Reverend Ethen Smith, as related in *The Ten Tribes of Israel,* they were sent to Cambridge. We are not told which Cambridge nor are we told who deciphered them there. However, the answer came back: they were indeed pieces of parchment containing passages written in Hebrew, plain and legible. The three remaining pieces translated as follows:

1. Quotation from Deuteronomy 6:4, 6

"Hear, O Israel: The Lord our God is one Lord: And thou shalt love the Lord thy God with all thine heart, and with all thy soul, and with all thy might. And these words, which I command thee this day, shall be in thine heart."

2. Deuteronomy 11:13-21

"And it shall come to pass, if ye shall hearken diligently unto my commandments which I command you this day, to love the Lord your God, and to serve him with all your heart and with all your soul, that I will give you the rain of your land. . . . And I will send grass in thy fields for thy cattle, that thou mayest eat and be full.

"Take heed to yourselves, that your heart be not deceived, and ye turn aside, and serve other gods, and worship them; and then the Lord's wrath be kindled against you, and he shut up the heaven, that there be no rain, and that the land yield not her fruit; and lest ye perish quickly from off the good land which the Lord giveth you.

"Therefore shall ye lay up these my words in your heart and in your soul, and bind them for a sign upon your hand, that they may be as frontlets between your eyes. And ye shall teach them your children, speaking of them when thou sittest in thine house, and when thou walkest by the way, and when thou liest down, and when thou risest up.

"And thou shalt write them upon the door posts

of thine house, and upon the gates: That your days may be multiplied, and the days of your children, in the land which the Lord sware unto your fathers to give them, as the days of heaven upon the earth."

3. Exodus 13:11-16

"And it shall be when the Lord shall bring thee unto the land of the Canaanites, as he sware unto thee and thy fathers, and shall give it to thee, that thou shalt set apart unto the Lord all that openeth the matrix, and every firstling that cometh of a beast which thou hast; the males shall be the Lord's. And every firstling of an ass thou shalt redeem with a lamb; and if thou wilt not redeem it, then thou shalt break his neck: and all the firstborn of man among thy children thou shalt redeem.

"And it shall be when thy son asketh thee in time to come, saying, What is this? that thou shalt say unto him, By the strength of hand the Lord brought us out from Egypt, from the house of bondage: And it came to pass, when Pharaoh would hardly let us go, that the Lord slew all the firstborn in the land of Egypt, both the firstborn of man, and the firstborn of beast: therefore, I sacrifice to the Lord all that openeth the matrix, being males; but all the firstborn of my children I redeem.

"And it shall be for a token upon thine hand, and for frontlets between thine eyes: for by strength of hand the Lord brought us forth out of Egypt."

These were the very passages the Hebrews bound in phylacteries and wore upon their foreheads or a wrist.

But these parchments were not found in a phylactery. They were found within a double strap of rawhide which was undoubtedly an ancient Indian headband. Long ago they were made in this fashion, a double or folded piece of

119

leather with a loop at either end through which a thong was passed for tying.

I remember well the night we stumbled upon this account. Suddenly, light burst upon us. I pulled off my headband and looked at it in the realization of a deeper truth. Very vain of our headbands we are, trying always to make them beautiful and expressive. No six-inch strap of leather, this. Made to encircle my head, it was solidly beaded. Still, true to tradition, I had woven into it the design I wanted my life to express—"all thoughts leading to the one God."

And then as the full implication grew upon us, we were saddened. At what point had our people lost the fullness of truth? We read the passages again and under those mighty words we saw the shadow of our customs from old times.

"There is one God—the Creator of all things."

"Only if we live by His laws will we prosper."

"Only if we love Him will He give His rain and His sunshine."

"Speak often of Him; in your councils, to your children and to the stranger among you."

And the firstborn! All children are at once offered to the One who gave them. But the firstborn son is somehow very special. He must be of all the truest, the strongest, clear of mind and clean of heart. Stories came to mind of oldest sons slain by their fathers when they failed to live up to the concept of morality.

To us, exploring in books, coming through the jungle of words upon words about our people, that moment of recognition was almost frightening—as though we had stumbled upon the grave of one of the Old People.

And we wondered—what happened to this relic?

Was it tossed back into the field once the question was answered? Stored in an attic with the arrowheads and tomahawks also found in the fields? Does it rest among the artifacts in some museum?

And who was "farmer Marrick"? Who deciphered the parchments? How we longed to unravel the mystery. So many questions forever unanswered.

Grey Owl was superstitious about this.

"It was found too soon, perhaps," he said. "Maybe it wasn't time."

CHAPTER 19

Black Hand Gorge

Some sixteen miles east of Newark, Ohio, on the outskirts of the small town of Toboso are the cliffs of Black Hand Gorge. The name still holds, though the curious black stained formation from which it arose is gone.

It was a familiar sight to early settlers. Many legends were told to explain the presence of the hand upon the rock, the favorite being that here was another of those cliffs over which the beautiful Indian princess leapt to her death for love and that her brokenhearted suitor cut off his hand and flung it upon the cliff.

There are many variations of the theme; but as always, the truth seems stranger than the fiction.

A Mr. Sherwood is credited as being the first white man to see the hand. He reported that in 1816 he saw the hand and that it pointed to a large mound a short distance away.

This was the era of canal building and in 1825 the rock was blasted to make room for a towpath along the canal. Thus the hand, which had stood in bold relief, disappeared.

Next came the railroad and the workers dug into the mound, taking great quantities of earth and gravel to build a road bed. And here begins the mystery that excited the interest of people in Europe and America. Brandt G. Smythe in his *Early Recollections of Newark* (pp. 59-60) tells of a paper read to the Muskingum Antiquarian Society.

A man by the name of David Wyrick was concerned about the ruination of the mound. He realized that soon it would be leveled to the ground and pass from memory. Mr. Wyrick was described as well respected in Newark, though uneducated. With the assistance of his son, he began to dig into what remained of the mound. The report to the Antiquarian Society contains this story.

"They [the diggers] were not long in their descent below the surrounding surface of the ground until they struck a rock. It was single and elongated. Uncovering it, they found the top was a stone slab. Removal of the slab revealed the skeleton of what was once a human being. While decomposition had been perfect, a mould covering the remains gave evidence of fibers as though the body had been clothed with a woolen garment.

"Under the stone coffin the searchers found another stone, or rather two stones, which had been joined like a box, about a foot and a half in length inside of which they found a tablet about twelve inches in length, and four inches in width.

"Engraved on one side of the tablet was an outline or profile of a man in the dress of a Hebrew, and on the other side were letters or characters which the finders could not make out.

"Thereupon they took the tablet to the Rev. Mr. McCarty, then rector of the Episcopal Church in Newark, for inspection.

"Reverend Mr. McCarty had the reputation of being a very learned man, especially as a student of the Hebrew language. He declared the lettering upon the tablet was in the Hebrew language, and after careful investigation deciphered them as being nine of the ten commandments.

"Matthew Miller, a minister of the gospel, who was greatly distinguished as a Hebrew scholar, was, at the time the tablet was found, engaged in New York, but his home was in Monroe township, this county [Licking County, Ohio]. Mr. McCarty submitted the tablet to him for examination, and he translated the lettering the same as did Mr. McCarty.

"The deep interest which was aroused in the country induced them to take the tablet to Cincinnati for further examination by a Hebrew rabbi, and he deciphered the letters or characters the same as did the other two ministers, saying, 'This is ancient Hebrew and probably antedates the birth of Christ many centuries.' "

The destruction of the skeleton and the fibers which covered it would cause a modern archaeologist to shudder. Today every inch of the grave would be examined, catalogued, and preserved. The bones would be chemically analyzed and the fibers would be identified. The whole thing would be dated by radiocarbon analysis.

But at least, here we have the expressed opinion of two named scholars, not to mention the Hebrew rabbi of Cincinnati. It would be nice to know his name and something about him. Was he the same man who deciphered the stone now in the Coshocton Museum?

In another account it is claimed that two stones were found at Black Hand Gorge; that at one time they were kept with other artifacts in a room used as a museum in the Licking County Courthouse in Newark. When the courthouse was repaired after a fire, the various articles were moved from place to place, and there was a possibility these tablets were sent to the Smithsonian Institution in Washington.

In 1882 about twenty miles from Detroit, Michigan, was found two feet under the surface a silver coin smaller but thicker than an American half dollar. One side represented a censer with smoking incense and a Hebrew inscription translated "Jewish Shekel." The reverse side also contained a Hebrew inscription translated "The Holy Jerusalem" with a tree, possibly an olive or date. The coin was originally in the possession of Dr. Duffield, Detroit. (At that time, the find was discounted because it was thought that the Hebrew alphabet was adopted from the Babylonian. It is now known that those who were taken by Shalmoneser in the reign of Hosea at least 721 B.C. used the present form of Hebrew letter. This antedated the Babylonian captivity.)

Published in *Alexander's Messenger,* Philadelphia, Pennsylvania (18-   ):

"A government officer stationed at Lake Superior, at an early day, before any white settlers had invaded that part of the country, after becoming acquainted with a number of Indian tribes, found one tribe in possession of a copper tube tightly soldered; and when asked what it contained they said they were not able to tell, but they had received it from their ancestors a long time ago. The officer finally prevailed upon them to let him open the article and when he did so he found it filled with parchment, with inscriptions that he could not read, but by sending the parchment to Washington City, where it was examined by competent Hebrew scholars, it was declared to be part of the five books of Moses."— Jenkins, p. 16.

Where are these relics?

CHAPTER 20

The Long Arm of Coincidence

Each tribe was divided into clans, and each of these had some animal or bird as its emblem or totem. None of these was an object of worship. Indeed, the Indian could no more worship an animal than he could another man, as all forms of life had shared equally as creations of God.

When the Indians encamped on a march, they always cut the symbol of their clan on a tree or rock to show they had been there. Sachems of each clan were a necessary part of all councils and affixed the mark of their clan to treaties as modern officials do a public seal.

For what it is worth, note:

Judah—a lion   Dan—a serpent
Issachar—an ass   Benjamin—a wolf

Like Israel, they divided a year into four seasons: spring, summer, autumn, and winter. This might seem a logical coincidence. It also might logically follow that the year was divided into lunar months.

But when one realizes that, as the Israelites, their ecclesiastical year began at the first appearance of the new moon at the vernal equinox, the arm of coincidence grows long.

Indians named the months from the ripening of the fruits of the land. The "green eared" month was the most holy, when the first fruits became sanctified and were offered up as burnt sacrifices.

In fact, it must be emphasized that burnt offerings were a prelude to many daily activities. The Medicine man or a woman, before going out to collect the herbs, roots, and bark from which he or she made potions, always burned tobacco and cedar shavings as a thank offering. Failure to do this would offend the Creator who had put these things on earth for man's benefit.

In cooking meat, either in the villages or on the trail, a little of the fat was thrown into the fire, not to the spirit of the animal, as some believe, but as a thank offering to the Great Spirit to whom all creatures belong.

Father Charlevoix, an early Catholic missionary to the Indians of the Lake region, left extensive reports about their habits and customs. Here follows his observance on preparation for war.

"He who is to command does not commence the raising of soldiers, till he has fasted several days, during which he is smeared with black, has no conversation with anyone, invokes by day and night his (sic) *tuteler spirit,* and above all is very careful to observe his dreams. The fast being over, he assembles his friends, and with a string of wampum in his hands, speaks to them after this manner: 'Behold! the Great Spirit authorizes my sentiments, and inspires me what I ought to do. The blood of _____ is not wiped away; his body is not covered, and I will acquit myself of this duty towards him.' "—Jenkins, p. 126.

130

Adair records:

"Before the Indians go to War, they have many preparatory ceremonies of *purification* and *fasting*, like those recorded of the Israelites.

"When the leader begins to beat up for volunteers, he goes three times around his dark winter-house, contrary to the course of the sun, sounding the war-whoop, singing the war-song, and beating the drum."—Adair, page 159.

When the warriors had all gathered the leader exhorted them to join him in sanctifying themselves according to their ancient law. Those who would follow him now entered the winter house where they lived entirely separated from their families for three days and three nights. Each day they fasted until sunset and then ate only sparingly. The seasoned warriors were diligent to watch the young and untried lest hunger tempt them to violate the fast.

During this time they drank of a concoction of bitter herbs kept in the Ark.

James Adair had ample opportunity to observe the Ark during the forty years he spent among the Indians. He was accepted as a fully initiated warrior, one of the few white men to have participated in the purification ceremonies.

"It is made with pieces of wood securely fastened together in the form of a square. The middle of three of the sides extend a little out, but one side is flat, for the conveniency of the person's back who carries it. Their ark has a cover, and the whole is made impenetrably close with hickory splinters; it is about half the dimensions of the divine Jewish ark."—Adair, p. 161.

Two men were set aside to carry and guard the Ark on the war trail. Their purification ceremony was longer than the rest. Their entire obligation was to act as its protectors and to act in the office of priest.

The Ark was never placed on the ground. It always rested on stones or pieces of log. It was deemed too sacred to touch either by the warriors or the enemy. In fact, many battles were lost that might have been won except that, when there was a possibility of failure, the first objective was to remove the Ark and its bearers from the desecration of enemy hands and the fighting became secondary.

A man who was at a conference of Indians at the Ohio River in 1756 was very importunate in his desire to see the inside of the Cherokee Ark. An Indian sentinel stood guard over it. As the stranger approached and appeared to try to touch the Ark, the Indian drew his bow and would have shot him had the man not beat a hasty retreat.

When Grey Owl read these accounts, he was astonished to learn that these things he had thought secret had been printed for all to read. He thought they were known only to the "Medicine societies" but agreed the accounts were accurate.

CHAPTER 21

The Burning of the White Dog

When I decided to write the story of our years of searching and of what we found, I wondered how to approach this subject. It had to be written or all the rest would be in vain.

And yet the old reticence of the secret, sacred things is so strong it stops the mind to think of giving up the last old knowledge of our guarded rituals.

Some things we thought the outside world had never seen, and we gathered them about us as ragged blankets, though we ourselves only half understood their meaning.

So I turned again to the old writings of Adair, Dupratz, MacKenzie, and the agent, Col. Johnston. I found that what we thought was secret had been seen by a number of people. The accounts were often garbled and the solemn, sacred character of the rituals often presented as cruel and savage rites. So I write of the events leading up to the most sacred ceremony of the year of our fathers and attempt to put the ritual into its proper context.

Spring when the first fruits were appearing on the land was the time of renewal. Throughout the village all was made fresh and clean. Old garments were cleansed or, too worn, they were discarded.

All quarrels between neighbors were settled. All sought out any they had injured or insulted and offered atonement.

Even the blackened stones of the council fire were removed and carried away.

From the people, twelve old men were selected to seek new stones to ring the council fire. They must be unbroken, unhewn.

When the men returned, it was time for the ritual to begin. Young men brought saplings and, thrusting them into the ground around the fire, they formed a bower by bringing the tops together.

Now entered the Holy Man robed in garments kept only for this time. White was his sleeveless robe, and white the swans' feathers on his brow. Upon his breast was tied a breatplate set with stones.

Indians! Remember their number!

Now was the time for the kindling of the new fire and upon it the Holy Man tossed an offering of tobacco and cedar shavings. Then turning to the people, he reminded them of their obligation to God and to each other and that they should remember they were His children and so live as to bring no discredit upon Him. Also, since they knew the laws of the Supreme Being, none should have to be reminded to obey the laws; if any had failed to prepare for the sacred ritual, it should be done now. If any were unclean in any way, they must leave so that the place would be holy and the sacrifice pleasing to God.

Came then the False Face Society, leaping and crouching in grotesque pose to drive out the last least trace of evil. When they had done, the men seated in the circle rose one by one and in dignity approached the fire to throw into it an offering of the first fruits of the season.

When all had made their individual sacrifices, and when all the prayers of thankfulness had risen with the smoke, there was a quiet pause. Then, consecrated to the task of purification ceremonies, came strong warriors bearing upon a cross made of branches the body of a small, white dog. Reverently it had been prepared without the spilling of blood or the breaking of a bone. Here to the fire they brought it and gave it as a supreme sacrifice.

And the smoke rose.

And in another place could be heard the laughter of the women as they prepared the feast of all the bounties of the earth, remembering to throw the first choice cut of meat upon the cooking fire.

Many years ago I asked my husband's father, whom I loved, why it was they burnt the little dog upon the fire and he smiled gently at me, answering, "Daughter, they had no sheep."

Brothers! In the book *Parker on the Iroquois* there is a translation of the Seneca prayer used at the White Dog ritual. Those who read it cannot help being impressed with its reverence; and it is good that men know that our people are reverent in their worship.

But there is a danger. The footnote says that it was recorded in 1906 and that leaves ample excuse for the impression that this ritual was but our understanding of a precept taught in the Old Testament of the Bible.

Bear in mind, as you recite the prayer, that the sacrifice was ancient when the white man came. In truth, it was practiced in secret for many years, because the white man's sensibilities were offended.

CHAPTER 22

Shadow Memories

Colonel John Johnston was delegated Agent of the United States to the Indians at Piqua, Ohio, July 1, 1802, and continued in that official capacity until 1830. Among those in his charge were Shawnee, Delaware, Wyandotte, Seneca, Munceys, and Mohicans.

The good colonel seems to have enjoyed friendly relations with the tribes. Apparently because of this and his determination to look after their interest he made many enemies, both Indian and white. Several attempts were made on his life, but he was always warned in time. Twice he made dangerous journeys through hostile territory to bring back people who had been captured.

It would seem that he was in a position to know his Indians.

He related that Black Hoof, the Shawnee Chief, told him he remembered playing as a boy in the tidewater of Florida. Also his people believed that white or civilized people had been there before them, as they had found trees and stumps long covered with sand bearing the marks of iron tools.

At the time of this conversation Black Hoof was eighty-five.

The Delaware also had a tradition, they told him, that their ancestors had come from the south and from west of a great river.

The Sioux are pictured as warriors of the plains, but they were much, much more than that. They were once a woodland people moving north and westward until they found the wild ponies and henceforth changed their mode of living. Once they were the Lakota, proud and noble.

Once they drove their canoes northward on the rivers, bringing shells and pearls and feathers to trade for the copper of the Lake region. They carried southward, too, flints from the Ohio country.

Their feet knew strange trails and their eyes saw the glory of the land southward.

We have forgotten so much. Our grandparents heard again and again the stories of the ancients. We watch television or read the books that profess to know the truth. It is only when we begin to assemble fragments of memory that a pattern begins to emerge.

There is much more evidence pointing to a migration from south to north than from north to south.

And in the customs and traditions of the American Indian, both South and North, we find startling parallels with Israelitish laws. Relics and stones and stories notwithstanding, however, few serious historians will admit the possibility of a connection. And actually, many Indians agree with them—not all believe the case is proven. Time after time, the tired old word "coincidence" is dragged forth to explain the similarities in the two cultures.

Consider the conduct of women.

Judging from the records, almost all tribes had laws

governing the conduct of women perfectly in accord with Mosaic Law. No attempt has been made to determine which tribes adhered strictly to this provision, but that the separation of women on certain occasions and at certain seasons was fairly general from north to south is evidenced from the sparse accounts and oldest traditions.

According to Dupratz the Southeastern Indians "oblige their women during their lunar retreats to build small huts at a considerable distance from their dwelling house where they are obliged to stay at the risk of their lives."

Among Indians on the northwest of the Ohio River, a young woman entering puberty immediately separated herself from the rest of the village and remained apart for seven days. During this time, the person who brought her food was careful not to touch her as she was considered unclean.

At the end of this time she bathed, washed her clothes and all the dishes or utensils she had used. She then returned to her father's house and was looked upon as fit for marriage.

A Muskogee woman delivered of a child was separated for three months or eighty-four days. *Crossweeksung,* an old Muskogee town, means "house of separation."

Women took no part in the Medicine societies, which were actually religious fraternities, nor in the sacred rituals. Many students have assumed from this that women were regarded as low creatures, but this is far from true. They occupied a position of high regard in all domestic affairs. A man who was unkind to his wife or children was looked down upon by all the people. Quarrels within a family were virtually unknown.

The Beloved Women were not in any manner a priesthood. They administered no sacraments, and certainly you would never have found them leaping about a fire in a miniskirt as moviemakers would like to portray it. They were old and dignified women who had learned over the years all the beliefs, traditions, and also the superstitions of their people. They were counselors for the people and diligent to see that custom was obeyed. And on occasion their advice was sought by chiefs and council.

The ideal woman was clean, modest, and soft-spoken. She was cheerful and loyal; and she was expected to grow in wisdom, directing her household efficiently.

It was said among some of the southeastern tribes that the book the white people have was once theirs; that while they had it they prospered and were happy. But the white people bought it from them in ancient times and learned many things from it, while the Indians lost their good standing with the Great Spirit. In spite of their lowly condition, He took pity on them and directed them to this country—that on their way, they came to a great river but God dried up the waters and they passed over dry-shod.

An old Christian Indian of Ohio told a missionary that circumcision was once practiced among Indians long ago, but their young men made a mock of it and the custom was discontinued. He also told of a tradition that the waters had once overflowed the land and drowned all the people living except a few who made a great canoe and were saved in it. While they were building it they lost their language and from that time Indians began to speak in many different tongues. The Indians to the eastward say that prior to the coming of the white people into the country, their ancestors were in the habit of using circumcision but latterly not being able to find any reason for so strange a practice, their young people insisted on its being abolished (Elias Boudinot, *A Star in the West,* p. 113).

The Hurons and the Iroquois had a tradition that the first woman came from heaven and had twins and that the elder killed the younger.

On the wall of an ancient temple in Central America is a mural. Here is First Woman; confronting her and reared to its full height is a snake. Her two sons are shown locked in mortal combat. There are two urns containing sacrifices. One is upset; the other is neatly upright, symbolizing acceptance.

CHAPTER 23

The Shadow of Pain

The story of the conquest of Mexico by the Spanish has been told often enough to need no recounting here. The violence born of war is harrowing to the mother of sons in any land or any generation. The enslavement of a people under conditions so terrible they begged for death is an awful thing to contemplate.

Sad as these things are, death passes and new generations are born. Children laugh again, youths fall in love, and eventually the green grass covers the graves.

But the Spanish conquistadores did one thing that was irrevocable—they burned the books.

They might have demolished the palaces and temples and carried off the gold, precious stones, and all the treasure; only the artist and builders would have mourned.

But they burned the books.

All of the history, all of the sacred writings, all the collection of human thought on which the race might have built again was routed out and burned in the public squares.

They burned all they could find.

How fast can one run with a book in his hand when

the soldiers come? How many crevices can one find in the mountains in which to hide the precious volume?

Those who risked their lives to hide the precious few are gone away. Only the memories remain.

In the 1820's family members descended from the old rulers of the land were grieved because the knowledge of their history was growing dim. They gathered together all the Old People and asked them to try to remember all that their Grandfathers had told them regarding their history. All searched their memories and then, comparing their stories so that only truth would be told, they began to compile the history of their race. When it was finished, they took it to the magistrate and had it recorded.

It began with the statement that their ancestors had come from the "region of Babylon and had Abraham, Isaac, and Jacob for their fathers."

Far to the north, on the shores of the Great Lakes, a Chippewa in a conversation with an early settler remembered sadly, "Once my people had a book, but we forgot how to read it and it was buried with a chief."

In the woodlands, around the campfire, stories are told of a time when we dwelt in cities, beautiful and shining.

And they say, Somewhere is buried the Book of Life and no man may seek it. It will come forth in its own good time; but what it contains of knowledge, who can say? Some believe it to be a genealogy that will forever establish our origins. Some say it is the Master Plan from the foundation of the earth.

But all agree it exists; it is a holy thing—and it will end all controversy.

CHAPTER 24

The "Savage" Indian

Something happened to the Indian in some far distant time—something so terrible it left a nation held for generations in a trauma. He does not know himself what the race experienced that closed minds to the directions and developments that would have fostered desires to build.

The culture of the Indian ranged from the very primitive foodgatherers of the far Southwest to the occupants of the well planned villages of the Mandan and the Iroquois who were preoccupied with law. Still, by today's standards or those of the mighty cities of Central and South America, the North American Indian appeared to be a primitive beginning the long slow climb up through barbarism.

And yet—there are evidences here and there of a link between the North and South. Relics are found throughout eastern North America that appear to have come from Yucatan. Tradition states that many of the tribes came from that general region. The attributes of the Beloved Prophet are identical with those of the great Ku Kul Kan worshiped by the Maya.

Cultural patterns underwent some unavoidable changes as the white man entered the picture, but early American statesmen were intrigued with the many facets of Indian belief and custom that were pure Israelite. Benjamin Franklin and Thomas Jefferson, among others, were convinced of a relationship.

Bancroft, in his book *Native Races,* seemed impressed with the many parallels of Indian and Israelitish custom though he made the statement with caution.

Early writers were convinced that the great civilizations of the south were descended from Israel.

Lord Kingsborough spent his life writing the volumes that, he hoped, would prove the point. He had been called a fanatic and accused of wordiness, but even Prescott, though he was skeptical of the idea, gave him credit for the thoroughness of his research.

Let us be content to say that there were certain parallels in ancient Hebrew, early Mezo-American, and North American beliefs, customs, and philosophies. We have to accept that either the North American had some communication with the South, or that he came from there; that either his roots were in Israel or that there were a great many coincidences.

If this is so and he knew in his past of the existence of great cultures and organized religion, how is it that he remained so long in such a primitive state and resisted so stubbornly all efforts toward civilization?

Let us examine what the "primitive" culture accepted—and what was missing.

Root and branch of Indian belief is the one Supreme Being—the Great Spirit, Father-of-all; creation is his. His name is too holy to speak; the names of his angels, his helpers, may be spoken.

The divine Son of Heaven, messenger from the Great Spirit, healer, teacher, Beloved Prophet and Rejuvenator is present in our beliefs.

So also is revelation to those who through fasting and prayer seek it. We may picture the sun, the rainbow, the elemental figures, but the Great One may not be pictured.

The same commandments laid down by Moses, though they are spoken in different words, were the laws of our villages. Except one law.

And it is the omission of this one that gives an indication of some ancient tragedy.

The more we study the ancient American civilizations, the more one common denominator stands out. They seem to have been obsessed with dates. On the stelae, or the temple walls, on the stairs to the temples—everywhere we turn are the ever present glyphs for Tun, Baktun, Katun. It was a science reserved to a powerful priesthood, and it is said they could measure time tens of thousands of years in the past or into the future. The science of this complicated mathematics was the business of the priesthood, but the public awareness of it would have been unavoidable. All of the people, all of the time, must have been conscious of the weight of numbers that regulated their lives.

If there were any link between the North and South, it seems reasonable that at least some of this should have rubbed off; but the Indian memory contains nothing to indicate a knowledge of numbers beyond the count of his fingers.

147

"When the world was young."

"Once, long ago."

"In the fullness of time."

Beautiful beyond numbers, he found these poetic expressions.

Mathematics, they tell me, is linked with astronomy. The North American Indian knew the stars and knew their paths in the sky. He marked the changes of the moon and the sun's position with the change of season. He developed no science of astronomy or mathematics from this, but gave thanks to the Creator for these guides and comforters.

So this is missing. You will find no dates. You will find no commandment regarding the Sabbath—though there are occasional references to an ancient and dimly remembered tradition of a special day of rest.

The other difference, of course, is the absence of permanent cities in the North. The Indians were a race with dignity, courage, and resourcefulness, qualities that might have produced a civilization, but which instead turned inward and produced a race of artists and philosophers.

Not all Indians were nomads. Many of them were able to support themselves quite well in a permanent location. Early white settlers were astonished at the size and varieties of corn, dozens of varieties of beans, and the maple sugar. The rivers were teeming with fish. Winter lodges were well constructed, warm, and durable. The longhouse towns were permanent settlements. Great stockades enclosed many of them.

One cannot look at the mounds without appreciating the incredible amount of labor that must have been involved in their building. There has been a tendency to attribute all mounds to a mystical race of so-called mound builders, but it is well to remember that in the not-far-distant past Indians were observing the Feast of the Dead. Their dead were gathered at periodic intervals and reburied until the mound rose high as a small hill. It was also recorded that in Georgia white men saw the SunChiefs standing on a "High Place" made of earth.

Perhaps the easiest explanation for the lack of permanent cities is to say that the Indian had not learned to build with stone. But if he could take a lump of hardest flint and fashion a knife blade or a perfect arrowhead, it would seem he should have been able to master the art of making a building block.

I have among my souvenirs a war-club head of Vermont marble. Very smooth and perfect it is. The ridges by which it was thong-fastened to the shaft are true and beautifully beveled.

But where are the temples which might have raised, white and splendid, from the skilled hands of the workers? From the morning to the evening the Indian was conscious of the presence of his God. His prayers were full of praise and thankfulness, naming each of the blessings provided by a loving Father for the children of men. Yet over the generations no powerful priest-caste arose to spur them to building great temples as other races had done. "Medicine Men" were spiritual leaders but confined their ministrations to their own tribes. The Beloved Men and Women were revered as mentors of history and were often a court of last resort in spiritual matters. Great prophets and teachers arose to reaffirm ancient values and formulate

149

doctrines that influence Indian thought even to the present day. Keen statesmen and some of the most fluent orators the world has ever known sprang from this "primitive" culture.

With mind and heart and skill innate, one might expect that the Indian should have advanced further on his climb toward civilization by the time the white man came. Instead, he looked with skepticism and distrust upon the fantastic rise of the cities.

Among my people, the storytellers spoke of the Ancient Ones in hushed tones. I recall we asked no question, accepting the tales as they were told. There was a feeling of old fears—of a terror too deep for screaming that had nothing to do with the stories themselves.

One thing impressed itself upon my mind. In our language we have no swear words; no way to take the name of God in vain, for his name is too holy for speaking. But there is one expletive that causes a gasp of horror, a hushed dismay. I have seen mothers strike at the angry child who voices it. The word is "snake." I cannot determine whether it is fear or awe we feel about this word.

We do not worship snakes nor are we unduly afraid of them. They are not symbols of evil to us; rather the conventionalized snake is our symbol for knowledge or wisdom.

Yet what is it that so stops the breath?

What could have happened in this land to allow the Indian to hold close the fundamental core of ancient knowledge and avoid like the plague building it into something more?

We have three points of reference—a reverence for the Supreme Being and his Holy Messenger; the old moral precepts; and a traumatic fear of the Ancients.

When the Spanish entered Central America, they found a land steeped in human sacrifice. We are told thousands of prisoners had their living hearts torn from their bodies to appease the Serpent God. Battles were fought for no other purpose than to provide victims. Still, sometimes there were not enough and the quota had to be met. In bad times like these, the priests were forced to dip into the local population to bring the sacrifice up to a respectable number.

Who would have been the logical choices? Not the kings and nobles surely; and certainly not the priests who were essential to the sciences of the day. Hardly the great artists and architects whose skill was needed for the building programs.

Poor little John Q. Public, that's who. It may seem romantic to imagine they trooped joyously up those stairs to the altar, but the old murals show candidates weeping tears of despair, and I think on the whole the victims probably took a dim view of it.

I feel sure that during this era, more than one little party slipped off into the friendly wilderness, perhaps forever to associate temples and cities, priests and kings with scenes too horrible to remember.

But this would account only for those who came late to the Northland. What of those whose traditions tell of finding people already settled in the mound cities? Historians say the mounds probably were built between A.D. 400 to 900. What was happening then?

In A.D. 300 the great Maya were at the height of what is called their Classical period. How beautiful were their temples and palaces. Life was prosperous, joyous, and they seem to have lived simple, moral lives with a great deal of ritual. Fruits and flowers were brought as gifts to their gods. Scattered throughout the land were many towns and villages whose simple artisans and farmers produced the necessities of life for the nobles and priests. There were those who hunted for brilliant feathers and soft furs, and miners who brought gold and jade and turquoise to make the cities and those who ruled them beautiful as the morning. In return, they received protection from the ambitious leaders that were already beginning to threaten.

There is a school of thought which insists that the great Quetzalcoatl, the Feathered Serpent, was no divine being, but a Toltec king whose terrible army moved upon the Maya about A.D. 900. For absolute carnage the tale of that battle has few equals. It is hard to reconcile the conduct of this king with the gentle attributes ascribed to the god.

At any rate, between A.D. 300 and 900 a great and terrible change took place. A race descended and was decimated. A gentle god whose symbol was the feathered serpent because he had power over wind and water was demoted and became a patron of arts and learning; and his symbol became perhaps the bloodiest god the world has ever known.

During all that period as the Mayan power declined a constant tide of battle flowed one way and another. And as in any other time and place many fled, only to turn and flee again.

152

Here, too, was terror.

But our legends tell of a time in the *North* country when the land ran red with blood and the people of the Serpent were involved, though whether as victor or vanquished, who can say?

There is only one account in existence that tells of a battle so terrible that the land "ran red with blood," as our traditions say; and that book is seldom considered seriously by scholars. Yet it was the tragic account in the Book of Mormon of that last battle that once and for all resolved our doubts as to whether it was indeed the record of the ancients.

There kneels for me forever that brokenhearted leader, weeping for a nation slain. And on another hillside other watchers, suddenly sick with terror and bloodletting, running blindly from each other.

Speak if you must of the Ancient Ones, but speak in hushed whispers. See them mistily as in a dream, for if you look too closely you will see what man can do when he builds with power.

Avoid the cities and the building of cities, for what man's inhumanity to man has done once, it can do again.

Avoid time, because somehow it is all bound up together—the temples, and the battles, and the measuring and preoccupation with time.

And as the children grow old and die and their children pass away, almost the ghosts are laid to rest. But sometimes the storyteller comes near the veil of memory, and the neck hairs rise.

A man stumbles and in rage mutters, "Snake."

And we tremble.

CHAPTER 25

The Extra Witness

When Grey Owl was quite a young man, someone told him that many years before, a white man had found beneath a rock some ancient writings that were supposed to tell the history of the ancestors of the Indian.

He often spoke of his fury at the audacity of a man who would dare to take what was put away for safekeeping—and in Six Nation territory at that! Steeped as he was in the belief that what was history was sacred to his people, it was some time before his temper cooled.

Meanwhile, he read the book.

Twenty years ago, when we began to see the weight of evidence that our legends and traditions were based on actual events, we planned to write a book that would be for Indians only. Perhaps because at that time our people knew such misery, we longed for the fulfillment of an ancient prophecy that we would at last "remember the wisdom of our fathers." We had to depart from the accepted trails of scientific research, for the legends themselves were outside the scientific pale. Then, increasingly as time went on, we were able to recognize in the pages of the Book of Mormon the footprints of the ancestors, dim yet discernible. The particular parts that spoke to us were not the points of doctrine. What we noted would perhaps escape the notice of theological students of the book. But a word here, a phrase there, awoke old memories of half-forgotten legends.

Now as I go about my lectures to schools and to historical societies especially, I find there is a continuing and eager interest in Indian philosophy. Almost invariably someone asks, "Have you read the Book of Mormon?" It is a dangerous book for those to read whose minds are closed. But since it was for those people whose interest was sincere and open that we decided to share the absorbing experience we had had in our search for the Ancients, we felt we must also share the witness of that book and its significance to our people.

Whether one is able to accept the Book of Mormon as divinely inspired, preserved, and translated does not alter the fact that it contains parallels with Indian tradition and custom that could not have been imagined by a farm lad in the early 1800's. At that time, the Indian had not emerged as a figure of romance. He was the enemy to be feared. He was the heathen savage to be converted. He was a primitive with no instincts higher than to survive. He was an ever present threat and an obstacle to civilization.

The Indian himself at that time was keeping carefully hidden any knowledge he might have had of any spiritual truth.

Some prefer to believe that the book was the pilfered manuscript of a work of fiction. There are certainly some questions that must be faced.

How can one explain the work of the descendants of the Lords of Totonicapan? How could it happen that in the year 1830, with the length and breadth of a continent between them, an untaught young man and a group of people writing a family history should express in no uncertain terms the same origin of the ancients?

The Indian has a testimony that at one time his people had a book which "they forgot how to read" or "buried with a chief."

Taken singly, the rituals of the spring sacrifice, the reverence for the Ark, the belief in one Supreme Being, unchangeable and unnameable, have been considered as coincidence—natural developments in man's religious experience. Taken all together, they seem to point to a race memory of the same origin as our own Christian religion.

Further, if all these signs were actively observed, one might argue that they were taught by some zealous missionary, but they are only shadow memories handed down by the "Old People." This argues for a very ancient heritage.

For those who are not familiar with the Book of Mormon, it purports to be the history of some of the descendants of the tribe of Joseph who set out from Jerusalem during the reign of King Zedekiah. Their offspring separated into two groups, the Nephites who were righteous and the Lamanites who were fierce and warlike.

As they were beginning their journey, it occurred to them that they ought to have some proof of their identity, and they sent some of their young men back to confiscate the family records. Compare this with the Lords of Totonicapan whose ancestors "came from the region of Babylon and had Abraham, Isaac, and Jacob for their fathers." One might reason that they had adopted this belief from the teachings of the Spanish priests, but it does seem odd that they also had sent representatives back to obtain from certain holy men "their titles."

A part of the book is an abridgment of the "plates of Ether," a people claiming to have made their way to the new world after the destruction of the tower of Babel. Though much of the historical sequence of Mezo-America seems to grow from one culture into another—as Mayan to Toltec to Aztec—there are fascinating glimpses of more ancient peoples who still constitute a puzzle to archaeologists.

The somewhat involved and rambling story of the dispersal of the mound builders told in the *Traditions of Dee-Coo-Dah* is reminiscent of the last battle of annihilation of the Jaredites as told in the Book of Mormon. If we place any credence at all in Pigeon's book it seems to indicate that although his Dee-Coo-Dah was Indian, he regarded his ancestors as separate and distinct from "those snake people" who later invaded from the south.

Though our legends were fragmentary accounts and the accounts of battles and migrations in the Book of Mormon long and involved, nevertheless they stirred old memories and gave us insight into our own history. And though we could not recognize the names of the leaders or prophets, the events and the prophecies were uncannily recognizable.

Dimly remembered in our past is the tradition that our ancestors came to this continent in great canoes and disembarked on a narrow neck of land; there we found other tribes with whom we fought many battles.

158

According to the Book of Mormon, the history of these ancient inhabitants was filled with warfare. There was a constant struggle to preserve the religion of the fathers against the unending efforts of the "ungodly" to destroy it.

In the end, all the Nephites were destroyed in one last great battle and their unhappy leader buried the record under a rock and went his solitary way, leaving the country to the savages.

One wonders then how any shadow of memory of the old ways survived.

There is one persistent thread that runs throughout the book that may shed some light and also explain why later generations of Indians had only vestiges of the ancient faith. There were intermittent periods of peace during which bands of Lamanites were converted to the religion of the Nephites. There were times of apostasy when groups of Nephites joined their dark brothers. Captives were taken, too, on both sides during the wars and undoubtedly among a people in such constant confrontation, there was some intermarriage.

Perhaps among the tens of thousands slain in that last battle were ex-Lamanites who had the ill fortune to espouse the right cause but the losing side. It may also be true that among those who joined the Lamanites, there were some whose spark of memory relit the eternal fire.

Somewhere a mother crooned to her child the praise of the Divine Prophet. Somewhere a Holy Man preached a return to the old worship and won converts.

The memories, both dim and bright, of hidden secrets handed down grow plain within the pages of the book. For best of all, there is the hint that there is more to come. The Book of Life? The faint remembered legend of a final and conclusive record so long lost?

And then there is the mind-expanding thought that we have other cousins scattered far across the earth, and they, like we, have heard in some forgotten time the voice of God, the Maker.

Certainly, beyond all else, the ancient authors had access to our prophecies and foresaw both our misery and our "dwindling in unbelief"; our vision of the Ancient Wisdom has grown dim, indeed.

As an extra witness, the book does explain much of the unexplainable in Indian history and philosophy. To the Christian, it reaffirms his belief in the universality of Christ. It affirms the justice and mercy of God in giving his universal law not to just a few, but to his children in other places.

If this be true, where in the world are the rest of the "lost"?

You Indians who may read this book, listen!

Here you have seen displayed for all to read the things you held secret and inviolate. Grey Owl and I also supposed that our sacred traditions were known only to our people until we read dozens of accounts by those not of our culture who had witnessed and written of them. Sadly, they saw only the surface and wrote as though these precious memories were evil. Truth is clean and good. It is time to remember and to unseal the lips.

Who are you, Children of the Great Ones? Where did the trail lead when you ran from the shining palaces? Did you travel so fast and so far you had no time to teach new generations the arts of building and fine weaving? Was the inborn skill of the silversmiths inherited from ancestors who worked the precious metals?

Did you build the high places in remembrance of the temple grounds?

And those of you who passed the walled towns—were there those who loved adventure and traded their settled lives for the long hunt? Did their grandchildren grow bored with the old tales?

How beautiful were our feet upon the mountains when America was clean and lovely. Sweet to slip through the forests in freedom and choose our own pattern of life.

It is our heritage, nonetheless. We are the sum total of all that happened in our past. The ancients were children once, born to mortal parents. Like a great river passes the generations of man.

The Hiding of the Sacred Harp

When questioned about their antiquities or their sacred beliefs, Indians shrugged off the historians' queries. There is a certain querulousness in early accounts when writers were unable to establish an intimate rapport with their subject.

Almost without exception the Indian cared not a fig what the white man believed. This was so appallingly insulting that it was much simpler to be convinced that he knew nothing at all about his past and therefore could not answer—especially since "everyone knows" that rather than speak a lie, the Indian will keep silent.

I heard the story of a colossal lie from an old man who had never learned to read or write. He had learned English from his grandson only to avoid being tricked or tripped up by the occasional "palefaces" he might meet. One might imagine from this that he hated all white men. Actually, he did not—he had a number of good friends "from the outside" and was genuinely glad of their visits—but he didn't entirely trust them.

"The white man has a different way of thinking," he would say. "It is very easy for him to change black to white—and he will only believe what he wants to believe."

To illustrate his point he told this story which, as is usual, he claimed to have heard from his Grandfathers. And also, as is usual in such tales, he often fell into the old picturesque language.

"They say that very long ago in a distant part of the country there was a great nation. The country was prosperous and beautiful and all the people were industrious and happy. They had great churches where they worshiped and the young were taught to read in the books, of which there were many. The cities were shining with every precious thing and could be seen from far off.

"Then some white people came and all was changed. At first the white people pretended to be friendly but soon they shot their guns and killed many of the Indians. They tore down the holy places and they destroyed the books and carried off the sacred treasures. Any who resisted had their hands or feet cut off or were blinded.

"They scoffed at the ancient wisdom and cut out the tongues of any they found worshiping in the old ways.

"At last they tired of all the violence and wanted to live in peace and to learn something about the people they had conquered, but there was no one who would tell them what they wanted to know.

"One of their holy men decided to take a young man into their company. They gave him new clothes and good food and treated him kindly for some time. At last they told him to return to his village and learn all the ancient beliefs of his people so that they might write them in a book. They wanted to know especially the beliefs of his people regarding the Great Spirit and the creation of the world.

"But the Chiefs were wise with much suffering and they said, 'We tried to tell them our beliefs long ago and they were angry and would not believe. Never tell the truth about the sacred things; tell them such a big lie that they will think no ignorant Indian could have made it up—this they will believe!'

"So the young man was instructed what he should say regarding the creation of the world and this is the story he was advised to tell.

"There were some crows walking down a dusty road, and, as crows will, they talked so much they had soon exhausted all their stories and grew tired of each other's company.

" 'It is too bad,' they said, 'that there are not beings to listen to our tales.'

"About that time they saw a cave and went to see what was inside. They came into the heart of the mountain and were surprised to see windows cut into the sides which overlooked a great plain. And there on the plain were men-beings all looking up. So the crows opened the windows and all the men-beings came pouring through them and out the entrance to the mountain.

"So was the world peopled."

The old man chuckled when I told him that this story had been solemnly reported to their king by the early Spanish missionaries. Try as I would, I could not learn where he had heard it except that it was a tale his Grandfathers told.

The early history of United States depicts the relations of the Indians with the French, the Pilgrims, and other settlers and records the wars that ensued.

165

The century before the landing of the Pilgrim fathers is rather sketchily drawn. Familiar are the names of the explorers—Ponce de Leon, Cabeza de Vaca, De Soto. But only students who elect to delve deeply into this phase of the conquest of the Americas are exposed to the brutality of their campaigns.

De Soto was with Pizarro in Peru and history credits him with attempting to control the excess of zeal on the part of the Spaniards. But having been rewarded in 1537 with the governorship of Cuba and the promise of a grant of land of his choosing on the mainland, he embarked on a tour of exploration of Florida with a force of 622 men.

He left a bloody trail. Up from Tampa Bay to the Savannah River—west and then south along the Alabama—north and west through swamps and forests to the Mississippi; across on rafts and barges, built with the failing strength of his depleted forces, on to the Arkansas and back again to the Mississippi where he died, ill and defeated.

The suffering of De Soto and his company was acute and he appears to have cast aside any sentimental qualms he might have had in Peru. The only question he was asking was "Where's the gold?" Finding none he vented his anger and disappointment on countless villages. Word of his coming was passed from town to town and, in the vain hope of receiving softer treatment, the Indians met him with gifts of food and rich furs. In return, they were bound in chains, maimed, or killed outright—or impressed into service as porters.

Once the invaders were led to a great mound upon whose flat top a crude temple stood. Great ropes of river pearls were festooned there and baskets full of them stood all about. The soldiers stuffed their clothes with all they could carry—and later threw them all away as they were valueless. The high places were desecrated and the temples burned.

If this one sorry chapter in the history of the Indian's experience with the early explorers were all, it would seem enough to check his desire to share the memory of the lost and sacred temples.

But it was not all. As the American settlers moved west of the Alleghenies, their curiosity fastened upon the mounds and endless earthen walls. They still believed the myth of "golden treasure." But if they could not find gold in reality, there was still some gain in compounding the "theories" that began to fill the shelves of libraries back East.

With what horror must the silent watchers have seen the half-decayed flesh of their recent dead torn from the burial mounds. How they must have cringed at the callous blindness of the white man.

The wonder is not that the Indian speaks so little of his ancient past but that he is able to confront his memories at all.

If the early settlers were human, they *must* have felt some guilt. Learned men of that time *must* have had some glimmer of understanding that another man's faith, though different from one's own, still is sacred and important to him.

In their guilt, men often rationalize away their weight of sin by self-deceit:

Put down the myth that these were brothers who

167

worshiped the same Creator—that thought is not to be borne. Substitute the myths of animal worship—of the worship of idols. Take the social festivals and translate them into occult religious ceremonies; then the guilt subsides a little, and one can hate the race to which these are ascribed.

Scatter and disperse the tribes, cutting them off from the Old Ones. Close the door on the past. And after all the books are written defining the "lore of the Indian," perhaps the conquered races themselves will believe the myth that they were ignorant savages without a faith until the white man came.

Now, in the fullness of time, the young men begin to hunger for the wisdom of their fathers—and there is none to tell it.

The memories are those of recent times when truth was covered. In the old dances and the old songs, we begin to grope our way toward the glory of the past. In the shadows stand the silent watchers, the Old People, shaking their heads in sadness.

There is, of course, that wonderful feeling of identity as the voices lift and the dancers whirl, or a blessing of peace in the ritual prayers; but the ancient wisdom of our fathers still is hidden. The branches of the great tree bear rich tradition as their fruit. The roots are buried deep.

Of late years though, here and there, our people feel the increased urgency of the Ancient Ones.

"Seek us," they cry. "Beneath the ritual and the legends is a deeper truth. It once was ours—hear us!"

Stark and terrible in its simplicity still turns the Sacred Hoop. Stripped of the embroideries by which it has been covered, the majesty of our Creator's covenant with his children blazes forth; for a moment we perceive that ritual is but the medicine-stick that prompts our memory of the basic, fundamental truth our fathers knew.

The Sacred Hoop! The rituals, the legends, tales, and dreams of many separated nations. Seeking, probing for the truth about our past, we have become somewhat like the woman who has put a paper somewhere for safe-keeping and now cannot remember what it was or where she put it.

Oh, brothers, hear the truth and mark it well! Listen!

Once the artist whose pictures grace these pages went to paint a mural at a great resort. On the wall in brilliant color grew a picture of the Mayans, quetzal plumes afloat above their brows and in full panoply of power. Suddenly as he painted came a quiet voice behind him.

"I am Mayan."

In a sudden fear the artist halted. So absorbed had he become in the subject of his painting, he was half afraid the figures might have spoken. But he turned and there behind him stood an Indian smiling gently.

"I am Mayan," said the stranger.

With what joy the artist saw him!

"Have I painted truth?" he asked him.

"It is truth," the Mayan answered.

All that day and through the night, the two men talked, comparing legends and traditions they had heard when they were children. Though the words were changed a little, root and branch, they were the same.

Suddenly there fell a silence. Both of these young men were students; well they knew the facts of history. One of them, the son of an empire lost and fallen, all its mighty cities covered with the jungle; one of them the offspring of a northern woodland tribe, savage primitives when the white man came.

Could it happen? *Does* it happen when people break the first commandment, go away from God, the Maker—set up other gods before him? Does it happen that the spirit of the nation falters, and the people fall from glory? Does it happen that they cannot live in peace together and their wars and their contentions leave no time or will to save a crumbling fortress?

In the South the jungle covers the remains of empire. In the Northland, too, an underbrush of borrowed concepts, misconceptions, buries deep the sacred truth.

How it happened still is hidden in our history. But I know there is a warning in the story of this people. For the two young men clasped their hands in kinship.

"We are brothers," said the Mayan.

"We are brothers," echoed the son of northern woodlands.

CHAPTER 27

The Cry of the Ancients

Let us tell the story of the Ancients—and let us tell it in the fashion of our people.

Far in the mists of time, beyond the days of legend, a people lived in a distant country who for one reason and another were especially beloved by the Creator. Perhaps it was that they were often unruly children and as a parent sometimes is foolishly fond of a wayward child, he often took them by the hand and told them of his love.

"Be good, my sons, obey my laws—and I will give you all the bounties of the earth."

And they would not.

So then he sent them forth to journey to strange lands—some here, some there across the world.

Some to the islands of the sea, some to the North, and others to the South.

And some at last came to a bright new land fresh as the morning. One would think that here at last old enmities would fade and brothers might share in all the bounties of their Lord.

But they would not.

Each, as its own kind emerged upon the earth, brought its old quarrels. The legends always say: "There were two brothers and they disagreed, and separated from each other; each went a different way."

There were those whose journey led them to a land of ice and snow. Hard was their lot, but it developed mighty men who sought the mountain of the North. Here brothers quarreled again and one with all his people went away somewhere and so was lost.

Some builded rafts and fragile boats and caught the ocean currents in the south. And oh, the land they came to! Rich with grain and fruits and native herbs and vegetables and meat and gold and precious stones.

One would think that brothers here could share the bounties of the earth and put aside all jealousy and strife.

But they would not.

The legends say there were four brothers and they quarreled. One went farther south into the land of stone. And one held fast the land they came to and became a mighty nation.

But where the others traveled, no man knows. Still, here and there they kept a sweet tradition. Each believed they were the favorite children of the Great One who had made them long ago.

Now lifted up in pride they built their separate lives, each fashioning with the tools of intellect and nature's gifts the life best suited to the territory.

And as it ever is with man, some built with power, made war, and captured slaves. They built great cities, roads, and temples shining in the sun. And each in time forgot that he was one of many. Each was the conqueror in his own realm.

Then came the visitors in ships with great sails leaping

on the sea. They came to trade. They brought strange stories of new gods whose rites were most exciting. They brought from long-forgotten lands across the sea their gods. The people followed after, adding others of their own until a mighty pantheon arose of Sun, and Moon, and Stars, and Death. The temples filled with priests and artisans who bore the common people to the earth with labor.

And now the exodus began.

Up from the South the Hopi came, into a harsh, unfriendly land and made it theirs. Up the Mississippi Valley streamed a band whose vision still was clouded with memories of how things ought to be. There must be holy places where the Sun would rest to eat the sacrifice. So they had heard. But here they built of earth, great Sun circles, mighty ziggurats and effigies. Here first were sacrificed at times and seasons the game they found in rich profusion, till in their zeal at last they gave the dearest gift of all, the blood of man.

Now in the South the Serpent stirred and cast his children forth in anger. Up from the South they came, running from terror. Bound to survive they were, avid for life. Who are these Others to block up the way of the Serpent? *We* are the chosen, so fight to the death till the land runs with blood.

Driven and harried the Mound Builders faltered. Back from their scattered towns fled the survivors. Captives were taken, absorbed by the Serpent. Ever his numbers grew, ever his strength increased.

Near the headwaters of the Great River, the last of the Mound culture gathered. Surely here was the place where their people might build again. Here a great dynasty rose known as the Eagle. Wise were the Chiefs of that last hope, the Eagles. Here they attempted to strengthen their forces. Here once again they besought the old gods for their favor.

Down from the North came the Coyote people, fresh from the mountains and skilled with the bows. They fought with their brothers, both Eagle and Serpent. Each had forgotten whose children they were.

Now in despair the Eagle departed, far to the South and West with all his people. He carried with him his Sun God, his ritual, bearing as well a deep and abiding resentment. Oh, for a place to rest. Oh, for a place to build. Oh, for a place where the Eagle might conquer the Serpent.

Now was a time of dark silence descending. Each tribe of the Serpent, each tribe of Coyote drew back in wariness each from the other. Each had been wounded and suffered much loss. Now was a time of division and the eyes and the ears and the tail of Coyote each kept their separate way forgetting the others. From each of the coils of the Serpent sprang a new nation, each claiming a part of the spoils as his own.

Here were the silent mounds, brooding and awesome; bury your dead where the dead ought to lie. Here were the walls, made for fortification; take them and use them if need should arise. Here are the high places; fear them, for here strange gods were invoked and strange magic was made.

How must the heart of the Great Spirit have broken, seeing His children divided and lost. No wonder visions arise in the silence.

These are the Ancient Ones. These are the "Grand-fathers" beyond the legends. These are the doorkeepers. They hold the key.

These were the ages when out of the silence of terror the legends arose. Those of Coyote exalted the land creatures, banished those of the water. The turtle is evil; alligators are lurking, awaiting the unwary. Monsters abide in the waters. Wind was their ancient friend. Sun was their guardian.

Serpent was kin to the creatures of water. Turtle and Beaver and Crane were the "Wise Ones." Wind was a "Flying Head" spreading much terror.

Now were the brothers divided in fact and in fancy.

Into this time of suspicion and distrust came the white man. Few in numbers at first, soon he became a mighty horde sweeping west across the land. Pain and pestilence and sorrow followed in his wake. And, in a hurry to reap the harvest of a bounteous land, he was quick to note the ancient enmity between the tribes. Though he had not the slightest notion of how it came to be—nor interest, if the truth be told—it surely worked to his advantage. For the legend rose that any Indian trusts a white man sooner than he trusts another Indian.

"See how the Indians die!" exulted the conquerors. "In a few years they all will be gone like the buffalo, the passenger pigeon."

But we would not.

Out of our misery—out of our falling down, out of our drunkenness, hunger, and death—here rose the prophets who saw in their visions old laws revived, and the people uplifted.

Handsome Lake, dying of alcohol, caught in his dream the old memory of truth. Here came the "Resurrector" and the four angels, teaching again all the precepts of honor. This was the old wisdom now called the Gai-wiio.

Far in Nevada, a poor Indian dreamed of a time to come when all the dead would rise, joyfully united again with their own. He dreamed of a bright being, Son of the Heavens, lifting his people again to the light.

Came then the wise Black Elk, the prophet. He spoke with the Ancients and knew the old wisdom. Then in his last years, in deep despair he prayed—not to the Sun or the Moon or the Bear, not to the Serpent-God, not to the Spider. Lifting his eyes to his Maker, he cried his repentance. Though much of the ancient religion had been given to him in his visions, now he confessed his failure to bring back the Sacred Hoop to his people.

Now again in these modern days a presence is felt. A young man riding alone in the mountains catches a glimpse of a silent watcher—one of the Ancient Ones waiting and waiting.

A young artist paints and senses behind him Old People watching and whispering: "Paint truth!"

This is the Sacred Hoop—an unending covenant. Not for our merits, for we have been quarrelsome, jealous, and unruly children. But in the majesty of the Great Maker, He will reclaim us—whether we will or not.

And we will.

CHAPTER 28

Little Pigeon to the Churches

We have come a long journey.

Present-day Indians grow a little weary with the sudden switch of their white brothers to a preoccupation with pseudo-Indian ways. They begin to wish that more people might be concerned with their affairs today. Many people who have grown up in Scouting, collected arrowheads, learned to do beadwork and perform the old dances seem not to have the foggiest notion of what is going on in the world of the Indian today.

Teachers say they have little information except that dealing with the Indian wars and early reservation days. It is as though the history of the Indian began with the coming of the white man and ended with the reservation. There they are—all the tribes arranged in their own little niches. The maps show them as they were when the first settlers came, each established in his own territory as though he had been there forever.

Up' and down and over and across the beautiful land went the feet of our ancestors. Clean wind and wide vistas entered their spirits and united them with earth and sky. Their Father sent the rain and sun and impregnated the Earth, their mother, who produced the food and medicines that sustained them, but the Indians are partners, too, in

177

this union. Theirs was the resourcefulness and skill that reached out to partake of the gift of life and they were completely adequate to this task.

Now there is a new system of economics. The Father who gave generously and the Mother who sustained are put aside and man stands alone to wrest from nature the means to support himself.

It is an alien concept for the Indian, and his economic misery for several generations past attests to his difficulty in understanding such a system.

But what of his faith?

It has been my deepest delight to be called here and there to talk about my beloved people—their history and beliefs, their attitudes and their problems. Knowing also the incredible joy of being part of the family of Jesus Christ, I long for the message of his truth to be brought to them.

I make no apology to those who are interested in the more historical aspects of our past for the inclusion of this chapter. If any believe they can have Indian history without Indian faith, they have missed the point entirely. If any Indian believes he can still retain his identity and become an unbeliever, someone has been leading him astray.

So, to those who believe that God's eternal law can change the world from darkness into light, I have something to say.

I can rejoice for our brothers and sisters in far-flung lands who respond to the call through our missions, but the Indian in me weeps—"Us too, dear Lord; don't let them pass us by."

The Book of Mormon says that in the latter days when it has been revealed, the message of hope will be taken back to the remnant of the seed. I cling to this promise.

One would think, if our people knew the background of this, they would leap to receive it. In truth, they do not often stay long enough to listen.

When we left our reservation almost twenty years ago, there were five churches of various denominations in a little over fourteen square miles of territory. Not all of our people went to church; in fact many of us were in a pretty sad state. Still, considering our numbers, the percentage of those who did attend regularly was about the same as would be found in any small community. Now two of the churches have closed permanently and others seem to be dwindling to a slow death.

This is not to say that all Indians have turned from God. God and his unchangeable law are inseparable from Indian thought. And I have felt with my people the heart-swelling emotion as we sang of Beloved Ye-Sos. However, I remember, too, the years both on and off the reservation when we were besieged by enthusiasts from many churches who claimed to "have the truth"—and found that all came short of the glory that our Lord promised.

Many Indians are returning to what they fondly regard as the "Native Church." Be very careful how you criticize this faith for I predict that when the worshipers at last come into a realization of just what it is they do, you will see a Christian church arise whose like the world has never seen. Still it is but a seeking and its tenets are not generally known, even among Indians outside the cult.

I have heard it expounded by young white cultists whose only understanding is that "they use Peyote." I have heard the older generation of Indians threaten to take it underground precisely because of that misconception.

Some years ago I received an invitation to attend one of the meetings. The enclosed circular indicated that the white man had taught untruths—that his religion had not brought hope and faith, but only deeper despair. From the points outlined, I seemed to recognize elements of the Code of Handsome Lake, portions of the old Pueblo worship, and overtones from the Sioux. And when I saw that the brochure was signed by an elder of an established church, I was confused and let the opportunity pass.

I have often regretted my decision and wished that I had gone to see how these various tenets were reconciled and to learn if perhaps there were indeed something in the philosophy that would lead the people to the light.

Perhaps the name itself is misleading, for to speak of a Native Church is to imply an ecumenicity we never had. Except for a common belief in the Supreme Creator and a dim race memory, our forms of worship were as different from tribe to tribe as are the churches with which so many have become disenchanted.

To sympathize with the problem of Indians who are seeking the true path, one must realize that they were a "captive audience" from way back who are just now reawakening to the fact that religion should be more than a sop—something more than an opiate to keep them quiet.

Missionaries had worked among the Indian people in the very early days of the exploration of the country, but when the dust began to settle on a sullen people on the reservations, a new era began. Things were different then. Churches had to apply to the government for permission to minister on the reservations. In order to be fair and not play favorites, the reservations were divided up among them.

That period was bad enough; it actually insulted the intelligence of the Indian. Offered were a few simple stories such as children might understand and periodic barrels of clothing—often feathered hats, evening gowns, and slippers in which he knew he appeared ridiculous. Also, he found it hard to reconcile the ideal of Christian brotherhood with the experiences he was having.

Then began the period in which the churches began to proselytize and the Indian found it strange indeed that there should be such division among those who claimed one Father. He knew only the old-time beliefs of his own tribe, and he never argued about the things of God.

Chief Spotted Tail, a Sioux, spoke on the confusion of the white man's religion:

"I am bothered what to believe. Some years ago a good man, as I think, came to us. He talked me out of my old faith; and after a while, thinking he must know more of these matters than an ignorant Indian, I joined his church and became a Methodist. After a while he went away; another man came and talked and I became a Baptist, then another came and talked and I became a Presbyterian. Now another has come and wants me to be an Episcopalian. All these people tell different stories, and each wants me to believe that his special way is the only way to be good and save my soul. I have about made up my mind that either they all lie, or that they don't know any more about it than I did at first. I have always believed in the Great Spirit and worshiped him in my own way. These people don't seem to want to change my belief in the Great Spirit, but to change my way of talking to him. White men have education and books and ought to know exactly what to do, but hardly any two of them agree on what should be done."

If this were all, my people might in time have come to realize that all good men seek good, and as they learned to read, they might have seen for themselves the path to truth.

But it was not all.

The sociologists moved in to "civilize" the Indian. Programs were formulated in Washington that, it was hoped, would separate him from his preoccupation with the "old ways." First to go was his dancing; government was displeased about that. He was led to believe that it was against the white man's law.

Next was Indian art. From ancient times many Indians had great talent for painting and regardless of what they painted, it came out as Indian. The beautiful sand paintings, the Yebechi on the Kiva walls, the landscape with a stylized rainbow in the sky—these were to be discouraged.

Then someone had the idea that if the children were removed from the influence of parents and grandparents, they would change and become "just like everybody else."

The missionary in his intimate position among the people was the logical one to implement these programs. Here again, I do not unduly criticize the individual preachers who came our way. Many of them were kind and well-meaning, and they saw physical and mental anguish no one in Washington could have dreamed of. Perhaps they really believed the end would justify the means.

But the collective sin that was committed was to take the Beloved, the Glory of Heaven, the Christ who rose above death, who could not weep for himself but who wept for man's inhumanity to man—this powerful Son of Heaven they presented as a meek little teacher only a little lower than the Indian agent. *He* approved the misery and hunger of our condition. Government was His boss. He wanted us to listen to Government even if it meant giving up our lands and our children.

It is going to take some doing to correct that frightful misconception of the truth Jesus taught.

I talked once to a lovely woman, educated and well groomed. She had a question to ask, and she wept tears of old grief.

"My father was Longhouse," she said. "The missionary said he would go to hell. Do you believe that?"

As I heard her story, I wondered.

When she was six years old the missionary came. The mother was converted at once. The father was not. She told me of the love they had for each other, of how dear and kind her father had always been; of his goodness to his neighbors and their respect for him. Remembering the strict moral code of the old Longhouse religion, I knew the sort of home she came from, where love and honor go hand in hand.

When they failed to convert the father, the missionary encouraged the mother to divorce him. This she did and went to work in the city. The children were separated in two different mission schools, and they grew up with this burden of grief and shame.

Now this child of Longhouse wept because she had begun to doubt the missionary's teaching and her father was gone.

Today a fresh new breeze is blowing. At both public and private powwows Indians are dancing again, bringing to joyous life the spirit of their people. Great artists are emerging, their work winning acclaim in the highest art circles. Poets and writers and sculptors are coming forth to express the beauty and the misery of their people.

And lest one imagine that this is all to be expected of the Sons of the Dreamer, consider the tribes that now conduct their own businesses, administrate their own school systems.

Still, the level of poverty is extreme—a type and condition of poverty unimaginable in the affluent land of America. Still the trend is for the young to try their luck in the outer world.

Statistics say that there is an increasing number of suicides among young Indians today. They were taught that the old ways are sinful and foolish. Do not honor the older people—they are total failures. They come out of their culture to find, not acceptance and fulfillment but violence, discontent, and fear.

They find they have traded the beauty of earth and sky and their own warm place by the fire for the well-known concrete jungle. And they find the "mess of pottage" less than savory.

What can be done to bring the truth to this remnant who are beginning to stir into waking? In other places a mission hospital or a school might be a start. This won't work for the Indian. All of his treaties "guaranteed" him these things as part of the price for the land. Even where these facilities are needed, he will not be unduly grateful if they are supplied, for he feels they are his by right.

There is only one way, and only you who are intimately linked with Jesus Christ can do it. With timeless love and infinite patience, begin at the beginning and preach the fulness of the gospel, having first understood yourselves what it is. It may be that this is the purpose for the "other sheep"; they force us as Christians to examine more carefully the depth of our faith.

Grey Owl was thinking of the agony of a people trying to be something they are not when he said, "The Supreme Being planted a garden here on earth. He didn't just make roses. We hardly expect a daffodil to look like a rose, nor the pine tree to become an oak, yet each is beautiful in its own way. So should we each blossom according to our design and so fulfill the dream in the mind of God."

Go to the Indian, not as to a mindless creature because he is different; his difference is precious to him—but he is still a child of God. He understands deep truths.

He has a quiet place where he can stand alone and very still, utterly and completely attuned to the beauty of earth and sky. So he, above all else, knows the great truth in the words, "Be still! And know that I am God."

He finds it much more possible to believe in a God who still speaks to His children through dreams and revelations than to accept a doctrine that says He stopped speaking to man many centuries ago. The God he knows is the "same yesterday, today, and forever."

When an Indian sins he does so without excuse. He may laugh about it, saying, "I learned it all from the white man," but he sins openly, knowing that he alone pays the price in loss of dignity and self-respect, and therefore sins against his fathers as well. He does not expect the natural laws to be manipulated to change wrong to right. The wisdom of long experience has shown him we live in a world of order, governed by natural law. Man breaks the law but does not change it. He has looked at the denuded forests and sees the coming flood, the extermination of species that brought the hordes of insect pests in its wake and made it "excusable" to release poisons into the air.

So he understands well the order of man's judgment of man. When one speaks of the downfall of Israel—or, as the case may be, the sins of the Lamanites—he may say in the words of Jesus, "Why beholdest thou the mote that is in thy brother's eye and perceiveth not the beam that is in thine own eye?"

In almost every city there are young Indians, many of them away from home for the first time. They are inclined to be shy and a bit unsure of themselves in your world. They do not know if you want them among you and they are often desperately homesick. They often fall into temptation; loneliness and the desire to conform to what they observe as the "white man's way" lead them to discover the easy camaraderie of the bars.

During my years in the white world, I have seen that those who would lead us down the path to evil are great "evangelists." They seek us out; they proffer their friendship. We do not stand outside waiting to see if we are welcome to their circles; they eagerly welcome us in.

186

But those who have light and life and hope to offer tend to draw closer into their insular little groups. All too often it is harder to drive an opening wedge than to get into an exclusive club. How long has it been since the lonely, the strangers, the unknown were sought out and the joy of witness shared with them?

Because of these things, we understand so well the commandment of Jesus: "Feed my lambs."

Perhaps after the generations of his silence, the Indian even has something to give.

I remember the Adventist pastor who was Grey Owl's friend—such a loved friend that he asked to deliver the eulogy at the funeral.

He spoke simply:

"I first saw Grey Owl when I was driving up Radio Hill. I saw ahead of me a man carrying a loaded sack on his back. I stopped to pick him up and by the time we had reached his little home in Jacksontown, we were deep in conversation.

"That was at 10:30 in the morning and the burden he carried was food for his children. At three o'clock we were still there—I enthralled as he taught me the glory of the Scriptures. I have had what is considered a good education in the theology of my church; I am well-grounded in my faith and had considered myself a fairly effective minister. But through the years, we tend to begin to mouth old sayings without stopping to consider whether they are really the teachings of our Lord or simply man's interpretation.

"During our arguments in the following years, whenever I began to get a bit stuffy in my thinking, Grey Owl

187

had a whip he cracked. That whip was the word 'Why.'

"It sent me back to the Holy Scriptures again and again and I began to see the truth of Christ's teaching as I had never understood it before. I loved this man, and I and hundreds of others are better Christians for having known him."

Now supposing you have considered all these things and decide you simply must be off to the reservation harvest fields. The single most important question you need to answer is, "Why?"

Will you go as some have done in the past thinking to find the Chief waiting on a white horse to usher you in to the councils? What then are you going to do if he meets you wearing a business suit and driving a Chevy?

Will you congratulate yourself thinking—as others have done—"Ah, here we shall have a nice prosperous little congregation"?

What will you preach when you find that he has already given not just a tenth but all his worldly goods to his neighbors, and the main reason he keeps his car is that there is no water within ten miles nor a doctor within thirty?

Or perhaps you are sincerely concerned about the "plight of the Indian" and go forth to free him from his "chains." What are you going to do when he laughs and says he's the only "free" person on earth?

Or you are going to sympathize with him for his past misery—and especially because he "lost" the country. Be very sure of your facts. He is likely to look you squarely in the eye and say, "Good! When are we going to get paid?"

Just as you of the outer world tend to prejudge all

Indians by one or two that you have known, or by old stories you have read, he will be inclined to listen to your talk of "righteousness" with a touch of skepticism. Missionary or not, you will be regarded as a "first class citizen" of a government that in the past has broken every treaty as it became expedient to do so.

Even now when able and educated Indian leaders are an accepted fact in the administration of Indian affairs, their people wait to see whether we are truly entering an era where righteousness and justice will apply to Indians, too.

If there is any common denominator among Indian tribes it is the interweaving of law and religion—and this in a way that has nothing to do with the separation of church and state. If you preach love in your religion and close your eyes to intolerance, this, to him, is mockery.

If you preach sharing, but only so far as it is convenient, you will be in misery on the reservation.

If you bring with you arrogance and churchly pride or vain and "simple" solutions to the "Indian problem," you are going to have problems of your own.

If you are inclined to sit back and think, We have Christ; therefore these people should ask for their dole of Christian teaching, you should read your Book again—carefully.

They are important, these Indians.

They are a key.

They are a minority of minorities.

They are "even these least."

But perhaps your motives are simply that you have found joy in the Lord and want to share your worship of him. Ah, there my brother, you have a chance. There are thousands of souls ready to join with you in worship.

So after you have fasted and prayed and dreamed your dream, pause and look back down the ages. Know that God requires not alone of the meek, meekness, but of the wise, wisdom; of the wealthy, riches; and of the powerful, justice and mercy.

Then go with strength, and the Son of Heaven go with you.

CHAPTER 29

Grey Owl to His People

What are we on this earth—the age-old question! A toy in the hand of some capricious mastermind? An accident of nature? Can we control our destiny, or is our every move controlled by fate?

"Precept upon precept; line upon line. Here a little, there a little. . . "

Is this the clue?

The cynics say with boredom, "Man must have a God, so he created one."

Is this true, or is it the final arrogance?

Is the Bible merely a collection of fables, or is it an absolute and indisputable truth that we in our conceit are too blind to see?

Can we, out of increasing knowledge, build a world sufficient unto ourselves?

Knowledge without wisdom can make a man a bore and a fool. We prove our power over the very laws of nature by building higher cities, bigger planes, faster cars—and a wind comes to wreak destruction. We conquer one disease and a new virus moves in to take its place. And still our knowledge grows and deepens, so swiftly we can hardly keep pace with our own language.

We look with pride upon our mighty feats, and someone comes along with a spade and we find that man has built before to such specifications as mock our present success.

We experiment with chemistry, philosophy, and all the ologies and we amass tons of facts and figures. And here and there a sage arises with a Theory. Sometimes it is a logical idea, and man goes trooping after the sage and lifts him up and worships the Theory that he has made. Then in the course of time, the Theory is proven false; the sage is cast down and called a fool. Still, some shred of truth is salvaged and added to new knowledge and a new theory, a new sage arises.

A shred of truth. . . .

"Here a line there a line. . . ."

And through it all, this ever mounting conglomeration of theory and fact, the Scriptures stand; no matter all the theories of scientists, geologists, historians; no matter the confusion of doctrine. Their history still unproven, their prophecies unbelievable—yet there they are.

Why?

Because the precepts are comprehensible to all ages of man? But they are not. The Bible is one of the hardest books of all to read. We become entangled in its "wherefores" and "verilys." Besides, it makes us uncomfortable. Besides, it says if you are good, the Lord will be with you; but look at the case of the neighbor who cheats on his income tax and beats his wife, and still has a better car than the preacher.

So we read and do not see. We hear and do not understand. We have an occasional flash as of something

194

deeper underlying the surface. We have even incorporated some of the laws of the Book into our customs.

Still we will not see, for we are man and there is none greater. We have made the past and with our great minds will mold the future.

But always and ever there is something missing. Ever some grain of truth is just beyond our reach, leaving the jigsaw puzzle of our knowledge just a little incomplete. We found a few pieces under the table, so to speak. Sometimes we had no language to describe the piece we sought. A few generations ago, who could have described infinity—earthbound as we were on our tight little island? Now we have widened our vocabulary to include eons of time—billions of miles—galaxy beyond galaxy. And we begin to have a glimmer of understanding.

So we return to the Scriptures and their talk of a God of Infinity—eternity. And we can no longer limit him to that tiny speck of land we call the Holy Land.

But then we stumble. How much of what purports to be the word of God can we believe, always assuming that he exists; for until the Scriptures are proven, we reserve some small doubt. We have our theories regarding the creation and the future of the world, and they seem logical to us; this Book with its threats and promises gives no scientific fact into which we can sink our teeth.

Or does it?

There was a time when the story of Abraham was suspect, a fable to illustrate a principle, simply because no such city as Ur existed upon the face of the earth. Then, of course, along came Leonard Wooley with his spade and dug away the dust of ages—and there was the city of Ur.

So, quickly, quickly the masterminds thrust the old theory into mothballs and threw together a new one. Well, yes, such a man might have lived in such a place and even *might* have had the intelligence to see that one God was better than many; but this foolishness about a covenant—a promise of protection and favor to the seed of this Abraham forever? Fable!

Where are the children of this Abraham, that we may see some evidence of this covenant? The Abiru are mentioned here and there in the histories of the Assyrians; we see them briefly on an Egyptian pillar; they are much in evidence at the height of Babylonian power; in later language we know them as the Hebrew and their unhappy relations with the Roman Empire are well known. In fact, their traces are so far-flung within the then-known world that one might be led to the impression that the seed of this Abraham did indeed become pretty numerous. Yet to our certain knowledge, somewhere along the course of history this prolific lineage, which must have comprised many tribes or family groups to be in so many places at once, seems to have shed some of its members, and the only Hebrews we can find identify themselves as the house of Judah. Of course, we have heard of that "fable" about the tribes of Israel, but there are theories covering that too. They were absorbed in the course of their many captivities. No one can explain why eleven whole nations *en masse* discarded their heritage, forgot who and what they were to the extent that not one soul was left to carry on their dearest principle—the purity of the line.

Well, at least let us deal with the house of Judah. We are not concerned with their beliefs about themselves; we are the skeptics and we are concerned with facts. And the facts destroy us, for the history of the house of Judah reads like a page from the prophets. We can lay the Bible beside the history of the Jewish nation and even the most confirmed skeptic must feel a premonitory tingle up his spine.

The cities, prophesied to crumble into dust and become the homes of jackals, did indeed crumble. The people of Judah were warned they would become a race of wanderers upon the face of the earth—and so it was. Slaughtered in their tens of thousands, despised and rejected time and again—in the Spanish Inquisition, in Nazi Germany, in the Arab nations, and in all the mean little souls who in hate choose, "Kill the Jew!" Where is Rachel and the tears she would shed for her children?

Wouldn't one think the whole sweep of history could have accomplished the extermination of such a fragmented nation? Yet here they are, trooping joyously up the hill to the Holy City. Crying for joy they come and fall to their knees to feel the ancient roughness of the stones against the forehead. And out upon the land they go to plow, to plant, to irrigate.

"The desert shall blossom like the rose."

One tribe accounted for. One tribe that has survived its direful prophecy and came into the promise. Though they wandered from each other and were lost to others of their race, here is Judah, alive and kicking, unexterminated, and unabsorbed.

History and prophecy!

Oh, my brothers, in all the world is there another

197

people who can understand better than you the truth of this precept? You, of all people, *know* there is a Father-God who set the stars upon their courses and who made the earth and all its creatures—including man. You have lived out your generations in the firm and sure knowledge of His presence and His love. If it were not so, you would have died as the buffalo. Tribulation has come in accordance with the prophecy, and the promise is just as sure. Is not this a covenant requiring only your willingness to live by His ancient and unchangeable laws to bring it to its fulfillment?

Then I speak sternly to you, my brothers, for many of you are being led away by false teachers. You have caught the disease of impatience. You blame the Christian churches and say that their religion is not for you. In this you are somewhat right. The narrow doctrine that lifts one line from the universal truth and says that this is all—truly this is *not* for you. For you, nothing but the wide and windswept truth of the Almighty God will suffice. But before you turn your backs upon the Scriptures and upon Jesus the Christ, before you trade one half truth for another, remember well the things of your fathers.

Now that we have learned to read for ourselves, my brothers, we cannot use the excuse that the churches teach false doctrines.

You have read the Scriptures and found them wanting? Then you have not read them with the knowledge of the history of your race as a magnifying glass.

Read again the first five books of the Old Testament. Read them to your Ancient Ones, for they were duplicated in our village habit from long ago. Read and recognize

Joseph, the dreamer, who sired a race of dreamers.

Read the prophecies of these latter days; they will speak to you with clear voices, you who have lived with dreams and prophecies.

Read the history as you would read the wampum.

And meet at last the Son of Heaven.

Have false teachers presented Him to you as a meek and lowly, small-time teacher confined to a small corner of Palestine? Or have you been led to believe Him another agent, enfranchised by the government?

In all fairness, we cannot blame Him if men have read this into His story. His ministry in that far-off land was so pitifully short; and of course, His friends and followers knew Him only as their dear Lord there in their own community. One brief line records His saying, "Other sheep have I not of this fold; I go to them."

Another says, "I have come to redeem Israel." Remember that word. "Redeem" means to reclaim; it does not mean to replace.

But all of Israel was not in that corner of Palestine. At that time, only Judah was present. The history of Israel ceased in 722 B.C. with the fall of Samaria. Israel was lost.

Lost to the world but not to God who knows, as Jesus says, "when even a sparrow falls." Perhaps He said more; we do not know. Perhaps His followers were much like men today, full of their own community troubles, and wrote only that which seemed "relevant."

But let us examine His credentials—His titles: The Son of God; the Great Physician; Wise Councilor; the Bright and Morning Star. The truths He taught are more

199

"relevant" today than anything that has been written since time began.

Love, truth, justice, compassion, hope, faith, wisdom.

We had better pause upon the threshold, for if we step across it we must leave behind all the sins that we have accumulated since the covenant was made. For what does it profit us to "remember the wisdom of our fathers" unless we remember the gentle kindness and concern by which the children of the Ancient Ones survived?

If there is among you one child homeless, cast outside because in this new world you "can't afford" to feed him . . .

If there is any old and frail and no young hands to cut his wood and bring his meat, no ears to listen to his tales . . .

If any neighbor deep in trouble has had to seek you out and beg for help . . .

If you have failed through slothfulness and idleness to use your mind and talents and your skills . . .

Or, if you have, and gained the wealth and rich possessions but find that you are now possessed by them . . .

Then you have failed to understand, my brothers, the truths that are your heritage and which were taught both by the old Belovéd Prophet and by Christ.

We must put aside violence; it was our downfall in ages past.

We must put aside greed; we know so well the misery it brings.

We must put aside hatred; for other men as well as we have stumbled.

We must put aside arrogance; this is a pitfall that has trapped many races. Just because we are a key does not mean that we are the whole house.

We must put away drunkenness and other lusts; we have no time, for we must be about our Father's business.

And now, my brothers, let us open that door.

Out of your legends, brighter than the morning, comes the Prophet, beloved of your fathers: Thunderbird, bringing the precious virtues as a gift from Heaven so that men might live in peace together.

"Truth, honor, wisdom, faith, patience, loyalty." To the old ones He was the Morning Star, "perfect in truth."

He had many names according to our various languages but always the memory is plain—a pale prophet with copper-colored hair and sea-green eyes and a beard.

Legend says He had power over wind and water and could command even the stones to stand upright. Sometimes he is found at the council fires telling stories of a land far away. And this is truth: we did not kill him. He left us in friendship, promising to return in the fullness of time.

Oh, yes, my brothers, the Scriptures are true—and Christ is true—but there is more. Our Old Ones also left a record. They left it in your memories and also in writings secretly buried, the history of their wanderings upon the face of this land—their wars, their kings and councils, and their encounter with Christ, the Beloved.

This, too, for your instruction read.

I believe the Book of Mormon, as it is called.

I approached it in anger that white men should have found it in its safe place in the earth and brought it forth. I said, "It is *our* history."

And then I read the words of that unhappy, lonely leader with his people dead before him on the plain— calling down the ages to the last, unhappy remnant of the seed: "Remember. . . ."

And because the legends and the prophecies have been like my daily bread in my life, I could believe that only by the power of God could our record be brought forth into the light of day. I am saddened when I find that those to whom it was entrusted tend to forget the purposes for which it was given; when they begin to substitute worldly power for the plain and precious truth. Nevertheless, the record is true.

And because it is true, because we insist that our fathers had been given truth from heaven, we stand in danger of His judgment when we quarrel about His truth.

What cruelties man has inflicted on his fellowman in the Resurretor's name: cutting of tongues, blinding, maiming, the death of children, the destruction of mind and memory. Such is the arrogance and conceit of the conqueror and the age-long despair of the conquered.

How dare you, Christian, war with Christian?

Worse still—how dare you, my brothers, catch up this bloody torch and war among yourselves? Christian or Traditionalist—who think you that you worship? Why do you divide yourselves over a name?

Over the mouthings of invective, over the noise of battle, comes the voice of the Son of Heaven: "Love your brother."

The seed of Abraham is scattered far and wide. And across the world our cousins stir and waken to the promise that when we open our hearts to the knowledge of our fathers—when we recognize ourselves for what we are and accept our obligation in the Covenant; then, oh then we will come out of our misery and despair, our hopelessness and faithlessness.

The voices of our Grandparents call to us from the dust we tread beneath our feet: "Remember God, the Maker, who made you brothers. Look back beyond the wars and hatred and remember. . . ."

So it shall be, when all our histories unfold in one unbroken scroll, we shall see the power and glory of truth so plain that others will see it through our reawakened eyes.

Then—as our prophecy foretold—we will climb to the mountains and lift wide our arms, crying with one voice across the world,

"Father! We are here!"

And He will answer,

"Israel."

Bibliography

Adair, James, *The History of the American Indians,* New York and London: Johnson Reprint Corporations, 1968.

Bancroft, Herbert H., *The Native Races of the Pacific States.* Five Volumes. San Francisco: 1883-1886.

Boudinot, Elias, *A Star in the West, or A Humble Attempt to Discover the Long Lost Ten Tribes of Israel,* Trenton, N. J.: D. Fenton, S. Hutchinson, and J. Dunham, 1816.

Brinton, Daniel G., (I) *The Myths of the New World,* New York, 1876. (II) *American Hero Myths,* Philadelphia, 1882. (III) *The Lenape and Their Legends* (Complete text of Walum Olum) Philadelphia, 1885.

Colden, Cadwallader, *The History of the Five Nations of Canada.* Two Volumes. New York: Allerton Book Co., 1922.

Colton, Alvin, *Origin of the American Indians,* London, 1833.

Cornyn, John H., *The Song of Quetzalcoatl,* Yellow Springs, Ohio: The Antioch Press, 1931.

Delafield, John, Jr., *Inquiring into the Origin of the Antiquities of America,* New York: Colt-Burgess & Co., 1839.

Dupratz, Antoine Simon le Page, (I) *History of Louisiana, Western Virginia and Carolina,* 1763. (II) *A Nation on the Mississippi.*

Edwards, Bryan, *History of the British Colonies in the West Indies,* Volume I.

Fowke, Gerard, *Archeology of Ohio,* Columbus, Ohio: Ohio State Archeological and Historical Society, 1902.

Hale, Horatio Emmons, *Iroquois Book of Rites,* University of Toronto Reprint, 1963.

Hansen, L. Taylor, *He Walked the Americas,* Amherst, Wisconsin: Amherst Press, 1963.

Harrington, Mark Raymond, *Religion and Ceremonies of the Lenape,* New York: ed. by F. W. Hodge, 1921.

Hills, Lewis Edward, *New Light on American Archaeology,* Independence, Mo.: Lambert Moon Printing, 1924.

Howe, Henry, LL.D., *Historical Collections of Ohio.* Two Volumes. Norwalk, Ohio: The Lening Printing Co., Public Printers, 1896.

Jenkins, Timothy R., *The Ten Tribes of Israel! or The True History of the North American Indians, showing that they are the descendants of these ten tribes,* Springfield, Ohio: Houck & Smith, 1883.

Johnston, John, *Recollections of Sixty Years,* Columbus, Ohio: Stonemore Press, 1957.

Kingsborough, Lord Edward, *Antiquities of Mexico,* Volume VII, London, 1831-1848.

Moorhead, Warren King, *The Etowah Papers,* London: Published for Phillips Academy by Yale University Press, 1932.

Neihardt, John G., *Black Elk Speaks,* Lincoln, Nebraska: University of Nebraska, 1961.

Parker on the Iroquois, ed. by William N. Fenton, Syracuse, N. Y.: Syracuse University Press, 1968.

Pigeon, William, *The Traditions of Dee-Coo-Dah,* New York: Horace-Thayer & Co., 1853.

Prescott, William H., *The Conquest of Mexico.* Three Volumes. Philadelphia: David McKay.

Smythe, Brandt G., *Early Recollections of Newark,* Newark: Thos. E. Hite Publications, 1940.

Squier, E. E. and Davis, E. H., *Ancient Monuments of the Mississippi Valley,* New York: Johnson Reprint Corporation, 1965.

The Titles of the Lords of Totonicapan, trans. from Quiche into Spanish, by Dionisio Jose Chonay; trans. into English by Delia Goetz, Norman, Oklahoma, University of Oklahoma Press, 1953.

Walum Olum or Red Score, trans. by Père Christine Rafinesque, Indianapolis: Indiana Historical Society, 1954.

Williams, Samuel Cole, *Adair's History of the American Indian,* Johnson City, Tennessee: The Watauga Press, 1930.

Suggested Reading:

THE HOLY BIBLE, especially:

Genesis 48	Leviticus 26
Exodus 24:4	Numbers 35:11-29
Exodus 28:6-21; 29-30	Deuteronomy 18
Leviticus 12	Deuteronomy 33
Leviticus 18	Joshua 4:2-7
Leviticus 19	I Samuel 21
Leviticus 20	Ezekiel 37

And, of course, John 10:16.